MEDITATIONS OF A PLUMBER PRIEST II

DALE E. MATSON

Copyright © 2011 Dale E. Matson
All rights reserved.

ISBN: 0615509967
ISBN-13: 9780615509969

PREFACE

"Great is the LORD, and highly to be praised,

And His greatness is unsearchable.

One generation shall praise Your works to another,

And shall declare Your mighty acts.

On the glorious splendor of Your majesty

And on Your wonderful works, I will meditate.

Men shall speak of the power of Your awesome acts,

And I will tell of Your greatness.

They shall eagerly utter the memory of Your abundant goodness

And will shout joyfully of Your righteousness." (Psalm 145: 3-7)

Mountains are frequently associated with God in the Holy Scriptures. Often it is a pivotal time in the history of God's people the Jews. Noah's Ark came to rest on *Mount Ararat*. Abraham took his son Isaac to *Mount Moriah* intending to sacrifice him. Mt Moriah is also the site of Solomon's Temple. *Mt Sinai* (Horeb) was where God revealed Himself to Moses and where the Ten Commandments were given. It was *Mount Nebo* where Moses struck the rock to provide water. It was *Mount Zion* where David built his palace and it was the *Mount of Olives* where Jesus delivered His sermon and where He was arrested. *Mount Tabor* is traditionally understood to be the place of His transfiguration. Even one of God's names El Shaddai can be translated "God of the Mountain" (NJB).

I was born and raised in Michigan where my family visited the Porcupine Mountains near Lake Superior in the Upper Peninsula. As a child they seemed imposing at about 1,600' of elevation. In the mid 1960's, a friend of mine, Dan McCosh, and I drove to California from Michigan in June and I saw mountains, real mountains, for the first time. As we approached Loveland Colorado, the Rockies emerged abruptly and immediately from the plains. My heart nearly stopped as we anticipated driving over Loveland Pass at nearly 12,000'. My hands immediately began to sweat. There was still considerable snow along the sides of the road as we crossed the Continental Divide. This view of the Rocky Mountains approaching Loveland made such an indelible impression on me that I knew someday I would live in an area where I could view and travel in God's glorious mountains.

In this second book on meditations, I have added several photographs taken in the central Sierra Nevada Mountains. In my twentieth year in Fresno CA, when the air is clear, I can see much of the central Sierra Nevada Mountains. The mountains offer year round recreation and I am there once a week.

There is no way to describe how my spirit is elevated each time I drive east into the mountains to begin a new adventure with friends or in the company of my Airedales Susie and Duke who change from pets to companions enjoying the winter snow. I also spent four of the best days of my life with my sons as we backpacked a portion of the John Muir Trail together. Hearing them talking together as men around a campfire as I fell asleep in my tent was as beautiful a sound as any waterfall or river.

This mountain therapy is where I fellowship with God too, for it was He who made these things and me also. It can at times be as intimate an occasion for me as when I offer the Great Thanksgiving in the Holy Eucharist.

I have included two selections, "Wilderness" and "My Testimony" from my previous book on meditations. May this mountain and wilderness theme set the tone for your meditations also.

Climb the mountains and get their good tidings. Nature's peace will flow into you as sunshine flows into trees. The winds will blow their own freshness into you, and the storms their energy, while cares will drop off like autumn leaves. ~John Muir

May God richly bless you,

Fr. Dale E. Matson

MEDITATIONS OF A PLUMBER PRIEST II

TABLE OF CONTENTS

1. Wilderness 1
2. Freud and the Denial of Guilt 5
3. The Law 9
4. Rain in Due Season 11
5. I'm Too Busy 15
6. To Remain on in the Flesh 17
7. Recovering the Image of God 19
8. Thomas Merton and Conversion of Manners 21
9. Grandchildren 25
10. Lex Orandi, Lex Credendi, Lex Vivendi 27
11. Forgiveness 29
12. Activities of Daily Living 33

13. Dangerous to Self/Dangerous to Others 37

14. Abortion: The Modern Holocaust 41

15. The Christian Church in Context 45

16. Cleansing of a Home 49

17. God be in my Mouth and in my Speaking 51

18. Lose Your Job? God Has Other Plans 55

19. Aerobic Meditation 59

20. Chad: A Humble Man 61

21. The Transfiguration 63

22. The Physician 67

23. The Ego and the Season of Lent 69

24. Bill Gates: A Failed Philanthropy of the Planet 73

25. Good Works and the Stewardship of Time 77

26. Elvis Has Left the Building 79

27. Seeking the Lost Part II 81

28. He Destroyed the One Who has the Power of Death .. 83

29. Therefore There is Now no Condemnation 85

30. Scripture: The Seamless Fabric Imbedded with the Gospel 89

31. The False Shepherds Who Steal Our Faith 93

32. Prescription Strength Jesus 97

33. What is the Gospel?... 101

34. Alcatraz and Anchorites 103

35. The Church of Fresno 107

36. Naps 111

37. What is our Daily Bread?.................................. 113

38. God's Omnipresence 117

39. A Prayer of Petition 121

40. Without Faith Works is Dead............................. 123

41. Hell 125

42. A Prayer of Intercession: Natural Disasters 129

43. Why I Got Off Facebook.................................. 131

44. The Final Stage Of Life 133

45. Sex, Drugs and Rock and Roll: Choosing Death........ 137

46. The In Between Times: Do Not Leave Us Comfortless ... 141

47. My Testimony 145

48. Evelyn Underhill: Mystic................................... 151

49. Stewards of the Mysteries of God 155

50.	The Didache	159
51.	What Must I Do To Be Saved?	163
52.	Only in Remembrance of Me?	167
53.	Ut Omnes Unum Sint (That they all may be one)	173
54.	Mountains	175
55.	Marathons	179
56.	The Fisherman	181
57.	The Church and the Homeless	185

ACKNOWLEDGEMENTS

I wish to acknowledge:

David Rippe for his photograph near Piute Creek.

My friend Sharon Madsen for the inclusion of her photographs in Toulumne Meadows, Mt. Whitney Trail View and the front and back covers.

My wife Sharon Matson for reviewing the manuscript.

The Cover Photograph is of Townsley Lake near the Vogelsang High Sierra Camp Yosemite.

MOUNT BANNER NEAR MAMMOTH LAKES CA

WILDERNESS

"I will make a covenant of peace with them and liminate harmful beasts from the land so that they may live securely in the wilderness and sleep in the woods." (Ezekiel 34:25).

While I live in a large city, Fresno California, I am also blessed to be within one hour of both Yosemite and Kings Canyon/Sequoia National Parks. I believe it is no accident that God is frequently depicted as being in the mountains or the wilderness. Although many of you may have gone on a spiritual retreat, probably fewer of you have actually spent time alone in the wilderness. It can be a singular experience to hear only the sound of your own breathing and the sound of your own eardrums. The wilderness can be stunningly beautiful and also brutally and tragically unforgiving if you are there unprepared. Be properly prepared for the mountains make their own weather.

The wilderness in Scripture is referred to often. It can be a location where God's people are tested and learn obedience. "How often they rebelled against Him in the wilderness and grieved Him in the desert!" (Psalm 78:40).

The wilderness can also be a judgment from God "I will Ezek 32:4-6abandon you to the wilderness, you and all the fish of your rivers; you will fall on the open field; you will not be brought together or gathered I have given you for food to the beasts of the earth and to the birds of the sky." (Ezekiel 29:12).

The wilderness is also a state of barrenness we are brought to, where we once again yearn for God. "O God, You are my God; I shall seek You [1] earnestly; My soul thirsts for You, my flesh yearns for You, in a dry and weary land where there is no water." (Psalm 63:1).

The wilderness is a place for a fresh start. "John the Baptist appeared in the wilderness [1] preaching a baptism of repentance for the forgiveness of sins." (Mark 1:4).

The wilderness is also an intentional destination where there is an expectation of encountering God. "But Jesus Himself would often slip away to the wilderness and pray." (Luke 5:16).

The wilderness is even a place where we can discover grace. "Thus says the LORD, "The people who survived the sword found grace in the wilderness--Israel, when it went to find its rest."

Whatever reason that may appeal to you, consider the possibility of time spent alone in the wilderness. It's not just a destination. Amen

FREUD AND THE DENIAL OF GUILT

If one takes the ten commandments of Moses or the great commandment of Christ as a summation of all of the rules, what is it that enforces compliance? Why do we usually do the right thing? Most would say it is our conscience that is our personal policeman and judge. The conscience is the internal judge that uses <u>guilt</u> to punish individuals that do not live according to their own internal rules. Jesus would compare someone who does not live according to his own rules to a house divided against itself and a house divided against itself cannot stand. In reality, guilt is a painful blessing if it causes us to repent; if it causes us to say, "I am sorry for what I said, for what I've done. Please forgive me."

Freud argued that neurotic individuals were really victims of social rules that were oppressive and unrealistic. These rules were internalized and created a conscience that was too strict and severe. The wish to express what Freud considered to be natural human desires was met with a scolding conscience. People hid these wishes from their conscience by pushing them down into their unconscious mind. Later the person developed mental and physical problems. It was the goal of psychoanalysis to get people to remember what they had intentionally forgotten. Intentional forgetting is called denial or repression.

Neurotics were encouraged by their therapists to release the undesirable thoughts from the captivity of the unconscious mind much as Moses led the Israelites out of captivity in Egypt. Like Adam and Eve attempting to hide from God, denial and repression are examples of a person hiding from his own conscience. The analyst or counselor is there to say to the individual, "It's ok to have those thoughts. You are a good person. You are just being too hard on yourself. You are suffering from false guilt. You are punishing yourself unnecessarily." The reality is that boundaries/rules provide freedom. The most freeing thing God did for the Jews in the Old Testament was not providing for their escape from Egypt but providing them with the Law. <u>The Law</u> gave them rules to live by and a life with meaning and purpose.

Here is where the priest should be taking a different path than other counselors. When it comes to the reality of sin, the Priest must not be "referring out". The psychologist, psychiatrist or social worker as a secular priest may claim that the individual suffers from false guilt but what about real guilt? They are enabling the individual to deny the reality of their guilt. They are providing a fig leaf and it doesn't work any better for those they counsel than it did for Adam and Eve. Unfortunately un-confessed sin and denied guilt eventually can give rise to physical problems (why is there such a rise in autoimmune disorders?) and accidents. In many cases self-destructive behavior is self-punishment. Here is the reality of what I am saying. We all have rules inside of us and as Christians we must live a life consistent with these rules. If we don't, we will experience guilt and guilt is psychological distress. Unrelieved psychological distress leads to physical and mental illness. Sin and its consequence guilt remain a reality in our time for Christians and non-Christians alike. Recent research indicates that one in five Americans is mentally ill. http://www.dailymail.co.uk/news/article-1331636/1-5-Americans-mentally-ill-joblessness-takes-toll.html. This is proof positive that a more permissive society with relaxed standards of morality does not lead to less neurosis. Freud was wrong.

It is not the job of a Priest to lower the conscience threshold in order to get rid of the conflict. We are here to <u>diagnose</u> the problem which is sin and <u>prescribe</u> the treatment which is repentance and confession and offer the <u>prognosis</u> which is absolution and forgiveness. What is needed is restoration to fellowship with God, our brothers and sisters through repentance confession and absolution. Unfortunately many clergy today have bought into the idea that people are basically good. If we are not in Christ, we are not "OK". Brothers and sisters, *we are not born basically good.* In Anglican and Orthodox Churches Baptism has included Exorcism; whether infant or adult. In the Roman Church we have the following: "During the Sacrament of Baptism, the Priest says two prayers of Exorcism".

On those occasions where we experience real guilt there is only one healThy response. "If we confess our sins, He is faithful and righteous to forgive us our sins and <u>b</u> to cleanse us from all unrighteousness." (1 John 1:9). Guilt is a symptom of sin, with sin as the underlying illness. For us, there is the weekly confession of sin and there is the Sacrament of Reconciliation. We hear the following from the BCP, "When the penitent has confessed all serious sins troubling the conscience and has given evidence of true contrition, the priest gives such counsel and encouragement as are needed and pronounces absolution." (p.446)

It has frequently been said that the couch of the psychoanalyst has replaced the confessional of the priest. The psychoanalyst has not replaced the priest because the psychoanalyst will not acknowledge the sin and guilt and cannot offer forgiveness on behalf of God. I know this from both personal and professional experience. I have more comfort, consolation and healing to offer as a Priest who is a representative of Christ than as a Psychologist.

If you are troubled with guilt and anxiety because of unacknowledged sin, there is a course of action that is the only remedy. This remedy is not found on the couch of the psychoanalyst. It is found in the church. "Therefore, confess your sins to one another and pray for one another, that you may be healed. The prayer of a righteous person has great power as it is working." (James 5:16). Amen.

THE LAW

"This is the covenant that I will make with them after those days, saith the Lord: I will put my laws on their heart, and upon their mind also will I write them; then saith He." (Heb. 10:16).

Boundaries/rules provide freedom. The most freeing thing God did for the Jews in the Old Testament was not providing for their escape from Egypt but providing them with the Law. *The Law gave people rules to live by and a life with meaning and purpose.*

As I wrote this statement for my Advent III Homily, it was as if a veil had been lifted from my eyes. It became clear to me that the Law is so much more than I had understood it to be. The distinction between Law and Gospel that I imposed on Scripture was a template provided by years of experience in the Lutheran Church Missouri Synod. This template created a contrast between Law and Gospel and whether Luther or Calvin, the purpose of the Law was in marked contrast to the Gospel. For Luther, the Law was seen as a Curb, a Mirror and a Guide. (Formula of Concord, 6th Article). Roughly put, the Law was a means God used to control men.

Why then is the Law portrayed in the Old Testament with the same adoration we hold the Gospel of Jesus Christ? Why does our Lord say, *"Do not think that I came to destroy the Law or the Prophets? I did not come to destroy but to fulfill. For assuredly, I say to you, till heaven and earth pass away, one jot or one tittle will by no means pass from the law till all is fulfilled."(Matthew 5:17-18, New King James Version)*

As we honor the Law, we are given life. As we honor God as commanded by the Law, we are given purpose. As we honor the Law toward our neighbors, our stony hearts are turned to flesh. As we honor the Law in keeping it, our priorities are established. As St. Paul points out in Galatians, "Therefore the Law has become our tutor to lead us to Christ, so that we may be justified by faith." (3:24).

The Psalmist mentions the Law twenty five times in the 119th Psalm alone. "I shall delight in Your commandments, Which I love. And I shall lift up my hands to Your commandments, Which I love; And I will meditate on Your statutes. Remember the word to Your servant, In which You have made me hope. This is my comfort in my affliction, that Your word has revived me. The arrogant utterly deride me, yet I do not turn aside from Your law. I have remembered Your ordinances from of old, O LORD, And comfort myself. Burning indignation has seized me because of the wicked, which forsake Your law. Your statutes are my songs in the house of my pilgrimage. O LORD, I remember Your name in the night, And keep Your law. This has become mine, that I observe Your precepts." (Psalm 119: 47:56).

It is not the Law contrasted with the Gospel. It was God's good pleasure to provide us with the Law that we could read and understand and love with the light of the Gospel. Amen

FRESNO COUNTY NEAR PIUTE PASS

RAIN IN DUE SEASON

"Then I will give you rain in due season, and the land shall yield her increase, and the trees of the field shall yield their fruit." (Leviticus 26:4, KJV).

There is a certain irony in the fact that the seasonal rainfall for the Central Valley of California is a meager eleven inches yet the Central Valley has the largest agricultural production in the United States. Some of the irrigation water is provided by deep wells but the Sierra Nevada Mountain Range to the east provides the explanation for how such an arid region can be so productive. Sierra Nevada is Spanish for Snowy Range.

The mountain snowpack is reclaimed moisture that has traveled east passing the Valley by and returns westward back toward the Valley as streams and rivers created by melting snow. The U.S. record for snowpack is at Tamarack CA of 37.5 feet. This melting snow is fed back gradually and is captured and stored in reservoirs that help regulate the flow westward toward the Pacific Ocean. These reservoirs provide recreation and electricity for millions of Californians in addition to water for drinking, irrigating agricultural products shipped around the world and providing habitat for wildlife.

The mountains provide natural containment of water reserves in the form of snow. When I hear the seasonal rain on my roof, I rejoice knowing that the Sierras are gleaning much of the remaining moisture from the passing storm and will give it back throughout the rest of the year. Much of California vegetation is green in winter and brown from mid spring until late fall. The spring reminds me of Exodus. "Behold, I will stand before you there on the rock at k Horeb; and l you shall strike the rock, and water will come out of it that the people may drink." (Exodus 17:6). In spring, the water literally flows from the granite cracks and the earth.

The rivers that flow out of the Sierras are spaced such that the entire Central Valley is supplied with drinking and irrigation water. The combination of mountains and the rivers to which they give birth, provide some of the most beautiful scenery on the face of the earth. Yosemite and Sequoia/Kings Canyon Parks are located in the Sierras and the rivers provide majestic waterfalls.

This is really a song of praise to God who is the Architect of this landscape. No engineer, artist, or farmer or could have even imagined such an intricate interplay of water, rock, snow and people. No one can describe this earthly beauty.

"The LORD shall open unto thee his good treasure, the heaven to give the rain unto Thy land in his season, and to bless all the work of thine hand;" (Deuteronomy 28:12a).

I'M TOO BUSY

"Come to me, all who are weary and heavy-laden, and I will give you rest."(Matt. 11:28, NASB).

I have heard the statement, "I'm too busy" quite often over the years. Frequently people will greet me with, "Are you keeping busy"? My response is, "I'm not into busy". In fact, God has commanded that we rest at least one day a week. The time God allots us is a resource and like any other resource we are obligated to be good stewards. In the church time is sacred.

I believe it is possible to be both spontaneous and disciplined. For example a musician is allowed a cadenza within a musical piece or a figure skater has a free program following compulsory requirements. In both examples however there is a matter of self-discipline. Without discipline neither individuals would have achieved mastery, no matter how gifted. It is a matter of prioritization of time.

So, why are individuals so busy? Why is life so often a matter of putting out a fire over here and heading to the next fire over there? There are a number of factors. "Busy" has a false prestige to it. Most people would rather be Marthas. It is a way of avoiding being intentional and attentive like Mary. It is also a means of avoidance and an alibi for poor or non-performance. Busy is a way to deal with anxiety and loneliness. People are good at filling their lives with distractor tasks. Multitasking is just a new name for busy.

I am not saying that time is somehow more holy in a monastery then on main street because it isn't. It is merely a matter of taking the time to listen to God the Holy Spirit speak to us in all things. It is including God in all of our activities in a continual silent dialogue. A Life lived intentionally for Christ is prayer without ceasing. A busy life that does not include God is a clanging cymbal and a noisy gong.

In today's world there is great pressure to live a busy life. Even taking a restorative nap is seen as a venial sin. Busy is not important; it is undisciplined. Busy is a lame excuse for interrupted conversation. Busy is mindless and anhedonic activity. Busy is form with no content. Busy is a vacant expression lacking ears to hear.

"Take my yoke upon you, and learn of me; for I am meek and lowly in heart: and ye shall find rest unto your souls." (Matt. 11:29, KJV).

TO REMAIN ON IN THE FLESH

Late in Paul's ministry, he wrote the following words to the Philippians during his probable first imprisonment in Rome. At that point he had only a few more years to labor for the sake of the Gospel. "For to me, f to live is Christ and to die is gain. But if I am to live on in the flesh, this will mean g fruitful labor for me; and I do not know which to choose. But I am hard-pressed from both directions, having the h desire to depart and i be with Christ, for that is very much better; yet to remain on in the flesh is more necessary for your sake." (Philippians 1:21-24, NASB).

I am at a point of understanding what St. Paul was saying. Increasingly I am on God's clock and no longer on my own. Through Christ I have accomplished every goal that I have ever dreamed. God has blessed me with too many gifts to enumerate. There is no longer any bargaining with God about delaying Christ's return. Bargaining is something that young persons can identify with. They have so much to accomplish; so much ahead in their lives. They have houses to build, children to raise, careers to cultivate. They are not ready to join with me when I say with John, "He who testifies to these things says, 'Yes, I am coming quickly.' Amen. Come, Lord Jesus." (Revelation 22:20, NASB). I am coming to a better understanding of the limits of my own strength as I age and the last years of my ministry are a similar kind of captivity to Paul. My health is no longer robust and my strength is diminished. Some injuries are chronic and pain is ever present. My confidence is diminished along with my senses. It is no longer about pleasure but about diminishing pain.

These are not the ruminations of a depressed person but an honest appraisal of my health and strength. The insults of life are cumulative and their weight increases with age. Christ does come as a thief in the night. It is He who binds the strong man that He may steal his goods. My goods have been unwarranted pride, self-reliance and a self-centered agenda. Paul's captivity letters (Ephesians, Philippians, Colossians, and Philemon) do not reflect his life situation at all. In prison Paul discovered true freedom, joy, contentment and riches in Christ.

Paul's answer to the dilemma to depart or stay was to stay because he knew that he was on Christ's clock, not his own. If you are imprisoned by pain, infirmity or loneliness please ask God what He would have you do in the time He has left on His clock for you. "I am crucified with Christ: nevertheless I live; yet not I, but Christ liveth in me: and the life which I now live in the flesh I live by the faith of the Son of God, who loved me, and gave himself for me." (Galatians 2:20, KJV).

RECOVERING THE IMAGE OF GOD

God created man in His own image, in the image of God He created him; male and female He created them." (Genesis 1:27, NASB).

St. Athanasius stated "God became man so that man might become God". Luther repeated this in his Christmas sermon in 1514. I think an important understanding of this is that to the extent to which we participate in the Divine nature and as Christ is formed in us (Galatians 4:19), the image of God is restored in us and we become fully human. Obviously, only Christ was fully human. None of us, even the saints become fully human on this earth. What does it mean to be fully human? I believe it is taking on the qualities of God like the fruits of the Spirit in Galatians 5:22. "But we all, with unveiled face, beholding as in a mirror the glory of the Lord, are being transformed into the same image from glory to glory, just as from the Lord, the Spirit." (2 Corinthians 3:18)

How much of our condition before the fall is recovered as we are Sanctified/Deified? We don't become "As God", we share God's qualities. Being fully human is a loss of self-consciousness and egocentricity but it is not the loss of personhood. It is not the annihilation of personality. We become incarnational as The

Holy Spirit dwells in us. It is having in us the mind that was in Christ Jesus. (1 Corinthians 2:16) In the words of Alexander Maclaren,[The notion of the indwelling Christ] "It is not to be weakened into any notion of participation in His likeness, sympaThy with His character, submission to His influence, following His example, listening to His instruction, or the like. A dead Plato may so influence his followers, but that is not how a living Christ influences His disciples. What is meant is no mere influence derived, but separable, from Him, however blessed and gracious that influence might be, but it is the Presence of His own Self, exercising influences which are inseparable from his Presence, and only to be realized when He dwells in us." I would add that it is also not cases of what people commonly refer to today as, "What would Jesus do?" (WWJD).

I believe the church has focused heavily today on what it considers to be the equipping of the Saints for service (Ephesians 4:12) but has neglected "…the fullness of Christ in Verse 13. The church could be convicted of child labor law infractions. Preaching today should resound with the basics of the person and work of Christ. What does it mean for Christians to be in Christ and what does it mean for Christ to be in them? This is restorative and transformative. This is not just Christ as Savior and Lord. It is Christ in you, the hope of Glory (Colossians 1:27). It is an awareness of the restoration of the image of God through the presence of Christ in all Christians. Amen

THOMAS MERTON AND CONVERSION OF MANNERS

The three vows of the Benedictine Monks are obedience, stability, and conversion of manners. Poverty and chastity are included in conversion of manners. Having read many of the Monk Thomas Merton's books, I have an admiration for him. He was spiritually brilliant and insightful. I am fortunate to have known him through his books and have known a couple of other men who influenced me through their lives. Although they did not shine with his brightness and were not as articulate, they lived the life he discussed in his writings and remain an inspiration for me. I will discuss them further in a short while.

Why does one become a monastic? It is accepting the call of Christ to follow Him. The vows of the monastics are an attempt to live out the beatitudes listed by Christ in His Sermon on the Mount. "Therefore we can conclude that we come to the monastery to seek Christ—desiring that we may find Him and know Him, and thus come to live in Him and by Him." (Thomas Merton, Basic Principles of Monastic Spirituality, 1996, Templegate Publishers, p.21).

"By conversion of manners we definitely consecrate our whole life to the service of God as monks, men who have turned their backs on the world, who have substituted the humility, chastity, poverty, renunciation of the cloister for the ambitions, comforts, pleasures, riches and self-satisfaction of the world." (Ibid, p.86).

The two other men I knew were not monks or oblates by intention but they were monks in their unspoken permanent vow of conversion of manners. Merton stated, "The vow of *conversatio morum* is a vow to live in the Spirit". It is aimed at spiritual virginity which is purity of heart. The point here is that the goal of monastic living is not seeking personal perfection. It is as Merton noted. "Christ is the center of monastic living. He is the source and the end. He is the way of the monk as well as his goal."(Ibid, p.9).

There is no reason to think that the intentionality of monastic living is a less distracted search for the face of God than a life where one is married, raising a family, serving in a parish church, living a disciplined and virtuous life, working in a vocation that provides meaning and seeing sacredness in ordinary existence. These two men were what I would call deacon monks. They took the church into the streets and into the workplace. They were Christ for their families. They were contemplatives who were also active. They were courageous leaders of others and helped form Christ in the novices. Their hearts were pure and their speech was unguarded. It didn't have to be guarded because they loved the people they spoke to. They only saw the good in others because their own hearts were pure. They brought out the best in others and gave them a hand up. They were innocent as doves and surprised at the moral failures in others. They were quick to forgive and easily brought to laughter. And why is this? It is because they had at a critical junction in their lives decided that Christ was the pearl of great price. He would be their head and they would live a life worthy of His unmerited grace to them. They were in holy orders and unaware of it. Their conversion of manners took place outside the walls of a monastery. Amen

GRANDCHILDREN

"Grandchildren are the crown of old men, and the glory of sons is their fathers" (Proverbs 17:6)

Jack be nimble, Jack be quick....now how does that go, grandma? The boys are over for a visit. I sometimes think it is a contest to see who can be sillier. I enjoy the mock scolding by them. "Grandpa, DON'T be so silly. Come and smell the chocolate on my breath. Meals are the best and worst time for me. It's like recess with food. "Grandpa, that's <u>not</u> snow on the roof, it's HAIL! Well *excuse me* for not being precise enough for a four year old.

I just had to check on them in the other room. From here it sounded like a tantrum but a quick check with grandma indicated it was only boys practicing wild animal sounds. I always ask them to make a noise like a rabbit. "Grandpa, rabbits don't make noises". Yes, boys that's the point.

We were up in the snow yesterday and they were both so excited about icicles. There is such a wonderment and innocence about two and four year old children. It's so fun to be "original" once again with "Don't eat the yellow snow". Sticks are also a necessary tool for working snow; for pounding it into submission; for reducing it to its basic crystalline structure.

Grandparenting children is kind of like riding a bicycle. Memories of my parenting experience seems to come back and inform me .... and yet it is not the same as it was parenting. Then it was a serious business and I was so different also. This is where the grandkids come to get dirty and have their toys stolen from them by our Airedales. This is where the hands of children and dog spit intermingle. This is where germs are used as grandpa's ally in making men.

When our house has stray toys, grandma is happy. They are like random reminders of her dear grandsons. (I have discouraged grandma from buying a license plate bracket that says anything about her grandchildren). For me, their toys are objects that I step on in my stocking feet. Jacks are especially painful. We walked the dogs in the rain today with the boys. They have their own pace. Very fast and very slow. Well, thank you Father for these boys. Their parents have just arrived and Grandma and I are saved once again from the kiddie monsters that never sleep, never nap and never tire.

"Truly I say to you, unless you are converted and become like children, you will not enter the kingdom of heaven."(Matthew 18:3) Amen.

LEX ORANDI, LEX CREDENDI, LEX VIVENDI

Our lectionary Psalm for the second Sunday after Christmas was Psalm 84, a Psalm of worship and praise to God. It wasn't until after I talked with our organist about the gradual hymn that she had selected that I realized that it was also based on the 84th Psalm. What struck me in particular was the last line of our hymn, "How lovely is Thy dwelling place". "...for thou shalt surely bless all *those who live the words they pray*." Immediately I thought of the Latin axiom Lex Orandi, Lex Credendi, Lex Vivendi which essentially means, As we Worship (Pray), So we Believe, So we Live. I would also add and so we become.

There is a more modern version of this concept, "You are what you eat" (Victor Lindlahr) but originally this concept was from the Liturgy and had both a literal and figurative understanding. "We offer and present unto thee, O Lord, ourselves, our souls and bodies, to be a reasonable, holy, and living sacrifice unto thee; humbly beseeching thee that we, and all others who shall be partakers of this Holy Communion, may worthily receive the most precious Body and Blood of Thy Son Jesus Christ, be filled with Thy grace and heavenly benediction, and made one body with him, that he may dwell in us, and we in him." (Thomas Cranmer, Book of Common Prayer, 1549).

The liturgy not only predated the Creeds, it predated the Christian Church. The liturgy was the form used for worship by the Jews in the Temple. The Christian church added primarily the Eucharist and Apostolic writings to an existing liturgy. Christians are the children of Abraham by faith and form.

There is an obvious reciprocity and interplay between worship, believing, living and becoming but it is this order which has fostered stability in the Christian Church and in the spiritual lives of those sustained by the Church. The first and great commandment is to Love God. It is God that provides the faith to believe and the reason to live. It is God that Sanctifies us in a life of service empowered by and dedicated to Him. A life lived in this order is rational, ordered, meaningful, efficacious, sacrificial, virtuous, prioritized, empathetic and unencumbered.

In the liturgy our personal and collective history is grounded in eternity. After The Gospel is proclaimed in the liturgy of the Word, we then have the liturgy of the table which contains the Gospel also. In the *anamnesis* we remember the atoning sacrifice of Christ, in the *epiclesis* the Eternal Word is reincarnate and in *reception* we experience reunion. We are in God and He in us.

The liturgy, the psalm and our lives have Selah moments that upon reflection are mystical and mysterious. There is an indescribable joy in all this. Amen

TAMARACK CREEK AREA

FORGIVENESS

"We remember today, O God, the slaughter of the holy innocents of Bethlehem by King Herod. Receive, we pray, into the arms of your mercy all innocent victims; and by your great might frustrate the designs of evil tyrants and establish your rule of justice, love, and peace; through Jesus Christ our Lord, who lives and reigns with you, in the unity of the Holy Spirit, one God, for ever and ever. Amen." (Collect for feast day of Holy Innocents [December 28th]).

This past Saturday a young man with a history of irrational behavior and a mission of evil shot and killed six people and wounded thirteen others. The most compelling image for me is the smiling innocent face of the youngest victim, nine year-old Christina Taylor Greene.

Our world today seems saturated with violence, a failed mental health system and incoherent responses from those who are charged with protecting and leading us. Where do we turn when our world seems to be in such chaos? In the end all we have is faith, hope and love as our prayers rise to God. That is how we express our hope and how we attempt to reclaim our joy. That is how we extend our love to those we cannot help in any other way.

This atrocity in Arizona reminds me of another horrific event. In October of 2006 a man took several Amish girls hostage. He shot all ten hostages, killing five and then he killed himself. What makes the incident in the Pennsylvania unique, unlike the tragedy in so many other cases, is the response of the hostages and the community following the murders. The Amish girls Marian and Barbie Fisher, 13 and 11, requested that they be shot first that the others might be spared. They were unafraid and Christ like in their response. The Amish community did not call out for justice knowing that it would only mend a small part of the huge hole rent in the fabric of the community. "The Amish answered the 'English', as they call those who live in the secular world, with their own generosity of spirit, even toward the Robert's (killer) family. Community leaders sent a representative to the family to express forgiveness. As donations came in from across the country to pay hospital bills, the Amish asked that a fund be set up for the Roberts family as well." (Newsweek, 10-16-06, P. 39).

The gunman's widow stated, "Your love for our family has helped to provide the healing we so desperately need. Your compassion has reached beyond our family, beyond our community and is changing our world"(Ibid).

In cases like this, justice when applied is an important but ultimately an inadequate remedy. It does not restore lives or even confidence in the system. It does not restore the hearts of those who hear of it. It is forgiveness that makes the circumstances restorative and transformative. It is forgiveness as much as any other virtue that demonstrates that Christ is being formed in us. As our anger subsides, let it be replaced by forgiveness.

"And we also bless Thy holy Name for all Thy servants departed this life in Thy faith and fear especially Christina Taylor Greene and those who perished with her beseeching thee to grant them continual growth in Thy love and service; and to grant us grace so to follow the good examples of all Thy saints, that with them we may be partakers of Thy heavenly kingdom. Grant these our prayers, O Father, for Jesus Christ's sake, our only Mediator and Advocate. Amen." (Prayers of the People, Rite I, BCP, p.330)

ACTIVITIES OF DAILY LIVING

"ADLs are defined as the things we normally do…such as feeding ourselves, bathing, dressing, grooming, work, homemaking, and leisure. The ability or inability to perform ADLs can be used as a very practical measure of ability/disability in many disorders." (MedicineNet.com).

While the Christian life is one of liberty as led by the Holy Spirit, it is also one that is conducted *decently and in order*. (1 Cor. 14:40, KJV). The passage is used most frequently when discussing the order of worship but it is primarily about the *witness* of worship. This can also be applied to life in general which is lived as worship. How do we offer witness to others by the way we conduct our lives? I am not just talking about the public witness of church attendance. Are we faithful in conducting our Christian ADL's?

I do not believe that a Christian led by the Holy Spirit needs to live a hectic, undisciplined, underproductive life. It is contrary to the life that Christ has given us. "I am come that they might have life, and that they might have it more abundantly." (John 10:10b, KJV).

The prayer closet part of the Christian's life is conducted as the Christian ADL's. Here are some ideas for the ADL's. How do you begin your day?

I rise early before the other occupants of the house awaken and begin with a daily devotional. It sets the tone for how the rest of the day is conducted and there are numerous devotionals available to choose from. Following this I journal the previous day's highlights and this also reminds me of things left undone. I include my dreams because God speaks to us in our dreams. My wife and I walk our dogs together and discuss our previous day and anticipated events of the current day. So much of remaining oriented requires a continual reorienting as we move through our day. I then exercise with various sport activities. As a part of my day, I make sure to connect with at least one friend and one relative. I don't mind being the one who usually initiates the contact. Meals are a great reason to get together. I am retired so volunteer work is helpful to others and necessary for me. However these ADL's were a part of my life while employed. My email and blogs are modern ways I also stay in touch with others and attempt to affirm or encourage them. I also attempt to write on a topic that strikes me each day and reframe a complaint into a statement of the desired end result.

What about travel? I take the same routine on the road with me. I have a travel journal that I can remove pages from and put them in my home journal. I take swimming goggles, bike helmets, running shoes, etc. with me.

These are my ADL's that regularize, standardize and organize an ordinary life. These are not measures of an especially Holy life. They are the measures of an ordinary normal

Christian life that continues to sustain me and those who God brings me into contact with including those He brings to my remembrance. I hope others never feel that I don't have time for them and that when I am with them; I am not paying attention because I am frantic to be somewhere else. "Come unto me, all [ye] that labor and are heavy laden, and I will give you rest." (Matt. 11:28, KJV). Amen.

DANGEROUS TO SELF / DANGEROUS TO OTHERS

"Let his mind be changed from that of a man and let a beast's mind be given to him, and let seven periods of time pass over him." (Dan. 4:16, NASB).

Jared Loughner murdered six people and injured fourteen others in Tucson Arizona this past week. This is another testament to our failed mental health system and is yet one more call for mental health reform. When the tipping point for treatment is *dangerous to self or others*, then it is no longer a mental health issue. It is then a legal issue and the police become involved. When psychotropic drugs were introduced they were touted as the panacea that would save the day. The drugs are not a cure and the individuals who need them frequently stop taking them. There are untold thousands of folks living with their families and on the streets. Their families have pleaded for help and hear the same mantra. They must be dangerous to self or others.

I can remember the parents of a schizophrenic son pleading with us to help their son who had just stripped all the paneling and drywall off their interior cabin walls as some kind of defense against the aliens who were sending him messages. When we advised his parents to notify the police they said, he is not a criminal in need of incarceration. He needs hospitalization and treatment. This is a common and tragic scenario for the families of the mentally ill.

I was involved at the county level in Wisconsin and was working in our inpatient unit the day it was permanently closed. It was a sad day for the families of the mentally ill. The idea was that it would be cheaper to treat them in Community Based Residential Facilities (CBRF's). So the mentally ill were passed from the state facilities (deinstitutionalization), to the county facilities to the CBRF's. The CBRF's were not equipped to deal with non-compliant residents and after wearing out their welcome in a number of CBRF's, they were given a bus ticket. We used to call it "Greyhound Therapy". Many of the folks that once had medical care; counseling and county services eventually had no access to any of these things. With the advent of the new system of crisis intervention and CBRF's, a new group of folks was gradually introduced into the streets along with those already there.

I worked for years with individuals, both adults and adolescents with mental illness. I believe there is also a new generation of mentally ill individuals who would have been marginally productive and capable of living independently except they compounded their difficulties with drugs. The drugs took them over the reality precipice and created individuals with chronic difficulties. I pray that we will reform our mental health system. Using the streets to house the mentally ill is worse than the intentional use of the expressways as ponding basins for excess rainfall.

There needs to be a reexamination of what constitutes adequate care for the mentally ill and how to fund it once again. As a blogging associate from Texas who also has a mental health background stated, "To what degree should we as a community let them slide into degraded lives on the streets? Underneath that question is a discussion about choice and personal freedom vs. the ravages of mental illness."

"For I was hungry, and you gave me something to eat; I was thirsty, and you gave Me something to drink; I was a stranger, and you invited Me in; naked, and you clothed Me; I was sick, and you visited Me; I was in prison, and you came to Me." (Matt. 25: 35-36, NASB).

ABORTION: THE MODERN HOLOCAUST

"Before I formed you in the womb I knew you and before you were born I consecrated you." (Jeremiah 1:5a, NASB).

I was at my weekly old guys' breakfast meeting today. We usually go for a bike ride following breakfast. One of our group members escaped the Nazis in Germany and we frequently talk about the horrors of the Holocaust. I mentioned a Washington Post news article from yesterday about the modern holocaust of the murder of live birth babies in an abortion clinic (not including the abortion of unborn babies) and it suddenly became silent. The next comment was, "Well, we should get going on our ride." What is this all about? I cannot believe there could be such indifference to this. This is not an unwillingness to discuss the unpleasant in general just the unpleasantness of abortion. Maybe it is because the group is all men and they have been told that it is not their business. Mainly I believe that talking about it would make it real.

A portion of the article stated, "Dr. Kermit Gosnell, whose abortion clinic was described as a filThy, foul-smelling 'house of horrors' that was overlooked by regulators for years was charged Wednesday with murder, accused of delivering seven babies alive and then using scissors to kill them."

My undergraduate university experiences included the awakenings of the ecological movement, God is dead and Paul Erlich's "The Population Bomb". His dire predictions ultimately led to our decision to only have two children (called Zero Population Growth) and a mindset that abortion was a reasonable approach to include in population control. At that time I had fallen away from church and was no longer a Christian.

When I returned to the church and rededicated my life to Christ, it was as if a light switch had been turned on and changed my thinking about human life in general and abortion in particular (It would take a few more years to conclude that capital punishment was also wrong and not consistent with being pro-life in general). After my rededication I didn't need a graphic exposure to the procedures or educational material. It was wrong for me unless the life of the mother was in danger. At the same time, as a crisis intervention worker I offered comfort to many women who suffered from depression on the anniversaries of their abortion.

The church needs to speak out boldly against the murder of newly born and unborn children. Any church that allows one of its leaders to call abortion a "blessing" simply because a woman has a legal right to make that choice is no longer a Christian church. A woman's right to choose does not supersede the unborn child's right to life. Scott Peterson was convicted of double homicide in the murder of his wife Laci who was also pregnant. This is because she had a human being living inside of her.

The unconverted mind may resist the truth about the sacredness of life. The mission of the church is to proclaim the

Gospel of Jesus Christ so that people can be saved. Saved people see things differently than before they were saved. We need to understand that a converted heart leads to a converted mind.

"And do not be conformed to this world, but be transformed by the renewing of your mind, so that you may prove what the will of God is, that which is good and acceptable and perfect." (Romans 12:2, NASB). Amen

THE CHRISTIAN CHURCH IN CONTEXT

"For in the multitude of your saints you have surrounded us with a great cloud of witnesses that we might rejoice in their fellowship, and run with endurance the race that is set before us; and together with them, receive the crown of glory that never fades away. Therefore, we praise you, joining our voices with Angels and Archangels, and with all the company of heaven, who forever sing this hymn to proclaim the glory of your name:" (Preface for All Saints, BCP, Holy Eucharist II.)

There is a view today among many contemporary church leaders that the church and its members are a product of the culture in which they are embedded. They are captives of context. Reality begins and ends with and on this earth. This view also shapes the churches' response to this same culture. The response must be culturally relevant and welcoming. Come one, come all. You may come as you are and stay that way. The message must be appealing and responsive to social needs. It must be sensitive, inclusive and affirming. It must be adjust to social change and environmental concerns. It is not a response to the command of God as much as human need. It is about the here and now of the material world. It is response driven by guilt and fear rather than love. It is serving others but not serving Christ in others. This church is devoid of sin, denies guilt, the need for atonement, salvation, faith, a God in Heaven, a divine and resurrected Savior and a Hell for those who chose to reject Him. There are no mysteries and miracles because there is no Spirit. All of the words are still used but mean what the relativists want them to mean. The meaning of words is based on convenience not truth. The Gospel of Jesus Christ has been replaced by many gospels for there are many ways. The gates of Hell will prevail against it for it is in fact not a Christian church. It is only a Potemkin village masquerading as a Christian church.

The Christian church and her members were intended to live in the world but were ultimately not citizens of it. If we mean by cultural relevance that the church takes on the values of society to obtain what is called today "street credibility" then it is nothing more than an adjunct social welfare agency. On the national level it is termed a "Religious Initiative" or "Faith Based Partnership". This church is an auxiliary agency of the government. On the international level this involvement is for some the "Millennium Development Goals" set by the United Nations. It is society setting the goals of the church and why not. Humans cannot escape their culture because they are culture bound.

The Christian Church and its parishioners however exist in a much larger context. It is not just local, national and international. We are also a part of the Kingdom of God. The Kingdom of God is eternal not temporal. It is universal in time and space and it is about the saving of souls and the worship of God. The context is without boundaries. Our community of faith has provided context for us through Scripture and Tradition. We are called by Christ and led by the Holy Spirit. Although we live out our life on this earth in a particular place for a finite period, we see ourselves embedded in the Kingdom of God that existed before the world was created and was brought to us here on earth by Jesus Christ in whom we also live and move and have our being. (Acts: 17:28).

CLEANSING OF A HOME

"Almighty and everlasting God, grant to this home the grace of your presence, that you may be known to be the inhabitant of this dwelling and the defender of this household; through Jesus Christ our Lord, who with you and the Holy Spirit lives and reigns, one God forever and ever. Amen" (Celebration of a Home, Book of Occasional Services).

My grandfather built our home and when he died and my grandmother moved, my father bought the home from his family and our family moved into my grandparents' home. My older brother and I slept in the same room and during the night I would sometimes awaken to see spirits hovering around. I would call out to my older brother who never saw them and was always irritated with me for awakening him. I don't know if I had sensitivity about this because of God's eventual call to Holy Orders but I have reflected on this and two other episodes in my life. In this case I believe that my grandparents who had embraced Mary Baker Eddy and the teachings of Christian Science had unwittingly encouraged these spirits to enter their home. After adolescence I never saw them in our home.

I was a visitor in a friend's home that had initially been a mansion then a nunnery then it was moved to a large vacant country location. I awakened with a feeling that I was being watched and the hair stood up on the back of my neck. I have never had this reaction before or since. My friend stated, after the fact, that they did have doors open that had been closed and a dog that would begin barking furiously during the night for no apparent reason. In this case I do not mean to imply that Roman Catholic Nuns who formerly resided there were the reason for this experience. I don't have any idea why this house would be affected.

I had a small home built in the early nineties and after moving in, had a similar sense that I was not the sole occupant in the house. It was as if I was a resident but not the owner. My spiritual advisor recommended that I light a candle and say a prayer in each room. She thought that it was possible that one of the construction people may have been involved in occult practices. After doing as she instructed, I became the sole occupant. I have lived in ten other locations over the course of my life without these experiences. In the house in which we currently reside, our priest at the time we moved in, offered the "Celebration for a Home". I also performed this for my son and his family in their home. It is fairly standard practice in both the Christian and Hebrew faiths to do this for the new occupants of an existing or a new home.

It is easy to pass this off as nonsense not fit for the 21st Century. I do not believe that it is and recommend that everyone take advantage of the opportunity for the blessing of a home. This is a service offered by the church.

"Let the mighty power of the Holy God be present in this place to banish from it every unclean spirit, to cleanse it from every residue of evil, and to make it a secure habitation for those who dwell in it; in the name of Jesus Christ our Lord. Amen." (Ibid).

TAMARACK HUNTINGTON IN

GOD BE IN MY MOUTH AND IN MY SPEAKING*

(*From "God be in my mind and in my understanding", p. 694, The Hymnal 1982)

I am totally committed to the idea that as Christians we are both asked and empowered to speak and in so doing, change the world in which we live. I immediately want to caution that this is not a "Name it and Claim it" theology that I am advocating. Biblical abundance is having enough (give us this day our daily bread). We are asked in our Lord's Prayer to call down the

Kingdom of God (Thy kingdom come). When we pray, we ask that God's will be done on earth (Thy will be done). God said through the prophet Isaiah, "So is my word that goes out from my mouth: It will not return to me empty, but will accomplish what I desire and achieve the purpose for which I sent it." (Isaiah 55:11). What does this mean? It means that when we pray the words God gives us, our prayers will effect change. The words have efficacy. His words will accomplish something. Prayers have no shelf life. The intercessory prayers of parents have helped their children after the death of the parents. We reach back to intercede for those who have passed on "And we also bless Thy holy Name for all Thy servants departed this life in Thy faith and fear beseeching Thee to grant them continual growth in Thy love and service." (Prayers of the People, p. 330, BCP).

Calling things that are not as though they were could be considered lying but in the context of faith it is a mustard seed sown from which an impossible situation can be changed. A miracle can occur because it is what God would have us say. Chronic unresolved circumstances are awaiting the prayer, "Thy will be done". Words have the power to help others heal. Each of us can remember something said to us that changed at a minimum the way we saw things. I can still remember my late mother saying to me in the midst of a crisis, "Son, tomorrow will be a better day". I can remember losing a job and a Christian friend saying to me, "God must have something better in mind for you".

As Christians we are called to be salt and light and challenged to confront a culture that hates God and yet needs God desperately. As clergy we are reminded that we speak for the church but as Christians we are all called to speak for God. In some cases this requires us to reframe a complaint or rumination into speaking or praying the desired end result. This is how our Lord prayed. We are God's ambassadors from His Kingdom inviting the people of this world to come there.

As Christians we can change our world starting with the words we speak. Our Lord is the Word of God made flesh and Scripture is the written Word of God. We are incarnational words of God. Paul called us living letters. By living holy and virtuous lives our words have the power to give life to others. Our words have the power to pull down strongholds, encourage others and change the world around us. Bit by bit, we call down the Kingdom of God to those who don't know they need God.

"God be at mine end and at my departing" (Ibid). Amen

LOSE YOUR JOB? GOD HAS OTHER PLANS

"Six days you shall labor and do all your **work**" (Exodus 20:9, NASB)

The late seventies in the Midwest were a difficult period with a deep recession not experienced in other area of the U.S. I was a journeyman plumber, heavy equipment operator and soil tester. These were skills that I presumed would always be in demand. The general contractor I worked for usually laid us off in the winter because the severe cold of Wisconsin winters sent concrete-like frost deep into the ground. We had a saying in construction. "We eat steak in the summer and soup in the winter (maybe)". Because of the recession, residential building nearly came to a standstill and I was not called back from layoff one spring. I had my family in our Ford Fiesta parked outside while I asked my boss for any job available including working in the lumber yard. He simply said there is no work and that I should look elsewhere. I was devastated and angry. Is this what being a new Christian is about God?

I had not finished my bachelor's degree because I had been drafted out of college my senior year for the Army. The past winter I began a degree completion program and had completed a course in developmental psychology. When we returned home there was an envelope in the mail box with my final paper and course grade. "The writing on my paper from the professor said, "This is the finest paper I have ever read by an undergraduate." It was an Epiphany for me. God was closing one door and opening another. I believe as it states in Romans, "And we know that God causes all things to work together for good to those who love God, to those who are called according to His purpose." (8:28, NASB). Another friend from church said to me when I informed him that I no longer had a job, "God must have other plans".

I am not attempting to preach a prosperity gospel here but I believe that a life dedicated to God will be directed by God. At the time I believed God was quickening a past interest in psychology which was my initial major in college. It was a difficult major and I had convinced myself at the time that I did not have what it takes to become a psychologist. Following not being called back from layoff, I took a job as a psychiatric technician at the county hospital. It was an entry level position at less than one third of what I made in construction. It was starting over but so was my baptism as an adult two years earlier. There was some financial help for veterans but the GI Bill had expired for me. I set my heart on finishing what had been started and found myself to be older than many of my professors. I still had doubts and the critical voice in my head had to be silenced with "I can do all things through Him who strengthens me." (Philippians 4:13, NASB).

I eventually wound up directing a graduate training program for returning educational professionals in School Psychology and school Counseling. They too were at a crossroads in their lives. How wonderful it was to hear each story and to welcome them into preparation for a new professional life. I was now a professor at a Christian university with a graduate school mission statement which included, "We are here to extend the Kingdom of God." As soon as the program prospects understood that God had brought them by crisis to this crossroads, they too saw the unseen hand of God opening a new door and closing an old one. Amen

AEROBIC MEDITATION

"Let the words of my mouth and the ***meditation*** of my heart be acceptable in Your sight, O LORD, my rock and my Redeemer." (Psalm 19:14, NASB).

As someone who completed two 100 mile runs people often ask me what I thought about during the time that I was running. My response is that I thought about everything and I thought about nothing. There is something about prolonged aerobic activity that not only produces endorphins, a naturally produced narcotic; it also produces a connection with nature and God. It provides a peaceful and righteous fatigue. As an ultrarunner, I would sometimes run, singing in the Spirit while moving along the trails. Trail running is part of the religious experience of the Tarahumara Indians of Northern Mexico. I don't want to single out running however, as the only aerobic meditation. Open water swimming, climbing a steady grade on a bicycle and cross country skiing are other ways that I have experienced this. There is a fundamental goodness about prolonged rhythmic movement.

You too may have been immersed in one of these activities in the context of a group as a form of social interplay where personal defenses were dropped and people discussed parts of their lives not shared with others at any other time. There is a healthy and playful vulnerability. It is similar to what is termed

"Free Association" in therapy. There is a similar transference and bonding. It reminds me of the experience of community at the communion rail during the Eucharist.

For me running has always been my drug of choice on a gently rolling trail through the woods along a lake. I hear the sound of my footfalls and breathing automatically timed by my steps. Running downhill on a single track trail elicits a rhythmic dance step to avoid rocks and roots. There are things about each of the other activities that appeal to me also. It is difficult to describe the joy of a good road bike with highly inflated tires on new asphalt and a tail wind. It brings an almost effortless ride where bike and rider become one. Cross country skiing is fast on a freshly groomed trail over new powder on a sunny day with no wind. It is wonderful to hear the squeak of poles striking cold snow. The ski strides are confident and one's balance sure. A fresh glide wax wards off sticky transitional snow as the day warms. Swimming is an adventure in open water, raising the head occasionally to navigate to a point on another shore. Occasionally there are glimpses of water birds or airplanes or even the moon in a sunny sky as the head turns to breath. Swimming is Tai Chi in the water. It is always a matter of working on the form. It is a complex coordination of discreet micro movements united in a common goal of moving forward.

These moments and movements are so very basic in a body God has provided for us. It is times like this when I am reminded of St. Paul's comments about our body being a temple of the Holy Spirit. I think about these holy acts of aerobic meditation, dedicated to God, being equal to the manual acts of the priest at the altar. For as we move, we move in Him, in whom we live and have our being. (Acts 17:28) Amen.

CHAD: A HUMBLE MAN

When people hear the name Chad, most folks think of either a Country in Africa south of Libya or an incompletely punched ballot in Florida in the 2000 presidential election. Today 03-11, however is the Feast Day of Chad, Bishop of Lichfield, 672. The Venerable Bede recorded that Chad was "a holy man, modest in his ways, learned in the Scriptures and zealous in carrying out their teaching." Bede also recorded that Chad kept the church in truth and purity, humility and temperance. The Collect perhaps best captures the essential nature of Chad. "Chad relinquished cheerfully the honors that had been thrust upon him." When told that his ordination was irregular, he offered to resign saying, "I never believed myself worThy of it."

In the Epistle lesson from Philippians for Chad, St. Paul states, "I have learned to be content with whatever the circumstances." (Chapter 4:11b, NASB). I believe that Chad and St. Paul were submitted to the will of God. This is not acquiescence or mere compliance. It is an acceptance. It is the end of grasping. It is the end of the desire to acquire more things to yourself, to adorn your ego with vestments to impress others.

The Collect also speaks to Chad's humility cautioning us to not think more highly of ourselves than we ought which is from Paul's letter to the Romans (12:3a). Thinking of yourself more highly than you ought is the opposite of humility. It is pride.

Humility is a virtue and Pride is a sin. Paul states in Galatians (6:3) "For if anyone thinks he is something when he is nothing, he deceives himself." The better we know our own hearts and ways, the less we will think in a condescending way toward others, and the more we will be disposed to help them with their infirmities and afflictions. No matter how insignificant men's sins seem to them when committed, yet they will be found a heavy burden, when it is time for the final judgment (Paraphrase of Matthew Henry).

Thus we have two primary things that Chad demonstrates to us by his life and service that when they are combined make a powerful witness to others, they are humility and submission to the will of God which yields a learned contentment. It is not the "I don't care" of those resigned to their fate. It is what God wills that matters and there can be zeal in submission to His will. It is not about the resistance to giving the church more of our time; it is about a willingness to give God all of our life. When I was baptized, the thought came to me, "You are throwing away your life for this Jesus". Yes, and each day that I am willing to do this once again, God can use me to accomplish his will on this earth. Unlike the U.S. Army slogan that calls us to "Be all that we can be". Pride requires us to be more than we are. This is a performance treadmill that damages us and those around us. Christ died and rose again that we can be LESS than we are. We become less so that He may become more. Knowing who we are is a matter of knowing who we are in Christ Jesus. It is knowing about ourselves as we are known. Amen.

THE TRANSFIGURATION

"Six days later Jesus took with Him Peter and James and John his brother, and led them up on a high mountain by themselves. *And He was transfigured before them; and His face shone like the sun, and His garments became as white as light.*" (Matt. 17:1-2, NASB).

In my sermon preparation this week I struggled with the temptation to use the Epistle lesson from Philippians (3: 7-14). In this passage Paul described his trials in such personal and human terms. He used "I" statements thirteen times in describing his total abandonment of his prior life under the law. He now, through faith, sought the pearl of great price, Jesus Christ wanting to know Him only.

However, the Old Testament lesson was a parallel account to the Gospel lesson with Moses on Mt. Sinai (Exodus 24:12-18), the Collect was about the Transfiguration and even the Psalm (99) talked about the glory of the Lord and His speaking from the pillar of cloud (v. 7). It is so much easier to understand, identify with and explain the struggles of Paul and even the human moments in the life of Jesus than it is to grasp the glory and majesty of God in the person of Christ. It is in the moments where the miraculous happens *to* Christ that He seems so different and unapproachable and we seem so unable to respond or even comprehend. Unlike Moses, His glory was not a reflected radiance.

In the story of the road to Emmaus in Luke (24:13-35) Jesus walked with two of His followers, "but they were kept from recognizing Him" (v. 16). It is only later in the breaking of bread that "...their eyes were opened and they recognized Him, and He disappeared from their sight." (v. 35). Jesus Christ is fully human and fully divine. Christ could make himself anonymous and once He allowed His true glory to manifest itself to three of His disciples. John and Peter both later wrote about the Transfiguration. John stated in his Gospel, "And the Word became flesh, and dwelt among us, and we saw His glory, glory as of the only begotten from the Father, full of grace and truth." (1:14). Peter related the following, "For we did not follow cleverly devised tales when we made known to you the power and coming of our Lord Jesus Christ, but we were eyewitnesses of His majesty. For when He received honor and glory from God the Father, such an utterance as this was made to Him by the Majestic Glory, "This is My beloved Son with whom I am well-pleased"– and we ourselves heard this utterance made from heaven when we were with Him on the holy Mountain." (2 Peter 1:16-18).

In the book of Revelation, St. John described another encounter with the Glorified Christ. "His head and His hair were white like white wool, like snow; and His eyes were like a flame of fire. His feet were like burnished bronze, when it has been made to glow in a furnace, and His voice was like the sound of many waters. In His right hand He held seven stars, and out of His mouth came a sharp two-edged sword; and His face was like the sun shining in its strength. When I saw Him,

I fell at His feet like a dead man And He placed His right hand on me, saying, "Do not be afraid; I am the first and the last, and the living One; and I was dead, and behold, I am alive forevermore." (Rev. 14-18a).

He is not only the friend we have in Jesus whom we love. He is the eternal glorious God who is awesome in His majesty and we fall on our faces in fear. He is so much more than we can ever imagine. Someday He will allow us also to see Him as He is in the fullness of His glory. May His holy name be forever praised. Amen

THE PHYSICIAN

"And Jesus answered and said to them, "It is not those who are well who need a ***physician***, but those who are sick." (Luke 5:31, NASB).

I was attempting to remove a tire from a bicycle rim last summer and noticed a strange pain in my groin area. Initially I didn't have the telltale bulge of a hernia but after about a week it was obvious that resting would not solve the problem. I had two existing hernias for more than ten years that were higher and asymptomatic. This however was not only uncomfortable at the site but there was a referred pain that was so intense I had to dismount my bicycle and walk home about a week later. There were other symptoms such as stomach cramps that I experienced for months but failed to connect to my hernia. I could still swim with little discomfort but I could no longer run or ride.

My prior surgeries were for a broken nose and a tonsillectomy. Both occasions were as a child and the ether experience was so traumatic that I believe I had Post Traumatic Stress disorder from it. Additionally I had severe hemorrhaging one week following the tonsillectomy. I also had general anesthesia for laparoscopic knee surgery with equivocal results. Thus, my attitude about surgery and surgeons was less than positive.

After months of struggle and pain, I met with a surgeon to discuss my options which at this point were limited to surgery. He seemed to me to be a confident young man which is a great quality for someone who is a surgeon to possess and it instilled hope in me also. We scheduled surgery for early January. I also knew that there would be a period of convalescence following the surgery even if the surgery were successful and there was no post-operative infection.

I requested and received an epidural anesthetic which eliminated the need for general anesthesia which remains an area of fear for me. As the surgeon began preparation for the surgery, I told him that his profession was probably second only to clergy for intercessory prayers. I don't recall his response.

So, what is the point of this? I believe there are folks reading this that need surgery but have avoided it because of fears of one sort or another. God has provided physicians for us as an intervention that is sometimes the only answer for disease or injury. I cannot describe the sense of brokenness, physical pain and psychological discouragement I experienced prior to my surgery and the sense of confidence that has returned since my surgery. Sometimes it is an issue of trust or fear that keeps us from making a necessary decision to even go to a medical professional. Sometimes it is a matter of admitting that there is a problem. Simply know that God has placed many professionals around us for our care. He works through them to care for us. Amen

THE EGO AND THE SEASON OF LENT

In our readings for the first Sunday of Lent, Adam and Eve were in a state of innocence before their fall from grace. God had breathed His life into them after forming them from the earth. They did not have an identity apart from God. They knew themselves only as God knew them. The idea followed by the act of disobedience led to their immediate loss of innocence and their sense of shame. They now had identities corrupted by sin that were estranged from God and a changed relationship with one another. Their shame was both an indication of a loss of innocence and the acquisition of self-awareness.

Self-awareness is an important developmental step in our fallen world but it is the result of sin. The rouge test can be used to demonstrate self-awareness at about eighteen months of age. If a child has rouge put on her face and is placed in front of a mirror, she will touch the rouge on her own face indicating that she recognizes herself as the person in the mirror. The cost of self-awareness however, is ego-centricity. Children are egocentric to the point of narcissism. Their needs and wants are the only thing that matters. Our parents, Adam and Eve, exchanged the rule of God in the garden for self-rule.

Hopefully, as we mature, we adopt a less egocentric lifestyle. Unfortunately, there are some who remain imprisoned in the narcissism of childhood. They are the folks diagnosed with organic or functional disorders. What the rest of us fail to realize is that even if we are not narcissistic, we are still self-centered and egocentric. We are still focused on and live in our own existential universe. We still see things subjectively through our own eyes and do what is right in our own mind.

What did our Lord Christ have to say about this? "Jesus said to them, 'My food is to do the will of Him who sent Me and to accomplish His work'." (John 4:34, NASB). "Therefore Jesus answered and was saying to them, 'Truly, truly, I say to you, the Son can do nothing of Himself, unless it is something He sees the Father doing; for whatever the Father does, these things the Son also does in like manner'." (John 5:19, NASB). ""I and the Father are one." (John 10:30, NASB).

What is the point of these verses? I believe that they demonstrate that Christ who was fully human and divine was always conscious of His identity in relationship to the Father. Because He was without sin, He enjoyed the relationship with the Father that Adam and Eve lost for themselves and us. As Christians, Christ is revealed in *us*, is living in *us*, is *being formed in us* and making His home in *us*. As *Christians*, we are to live a crucified life. Lent is the time to put off the old self (Colossians 3:12) the egocentric self and to put on the new self (Ephesians 4:24). Our real and authentic self is hidden in Christ and "In Him we live and move and exist." (Acts 17:28a, NASB). As we are transformed into Christ through the sanctifying power of the Holy Spirit, we shall again know ourselves as we are known. This is living the born again life with access to Christ who is the vine and the tree of life. Amen

BILL GATES: A FAILED PHILANTHROPY FOR THE PLANET

"And God blessed them. And God said to them, 'Be fruitful and multiply and fill the earth and subdue it and have dominion over the fish of the sea and over the birds of the heavens and over every living thing that moves on the earth'." (Genesis 1:28)

"I'd like to share a revelation I've had during my time here. It came to me when I tried to classify your species. I realized that you're not

actually mammals. Every mammal on this planet instinctively develops a natural equilibrium with their surrounding environment, but you humans do not. You move to an area, and you multiply, and you multiply, until every natural resource is consumed. The only way you can survive is to spread to another area. There is another organism on this planet that follows the same pattern. Do you know what it is? A virus. Human beings are a disease, a cancer of this planet. You are a plague, and we ... are the cure. (Agent Smith speaking to Morpheus in the movie "The Matrix")

"One of the world's wealthiest men and the founder of Microsoft, Bill Gates, has suggested vaccines as one method of reducing the world's population. Gates made his remarks to the invitation-only Technology, Entertainment and Design 2010 Conference in Long Beach, Calif. His February address was titled, "Innovating to Zero!" He presented a speech on global warming, stating that CO_2 emissions must be reduced to zero by 2050. Gates said every person on the planet puts out an average of about five tons of CO_2 per year. "Somehow we have to make changes that will bring that down to zero," he said. "It's been constantly going up." http://www.wnd.com/?pageId=127346.

Bill Gates would probably see himself as a major contributor to humanitarian causes in third world countries. He is a man with enormous financial clout who is attempting to literally change the face of our planet. I am not prepared to argue whether increased CO_2 increases temperature or the reverse. I am also not prepared to argue whether humans are major or only minor contributors to CO_2 emissions. I am here to argue against what seems to be a counterintuitive rationale that increased immunization will lead to less mortality and less population. In his 2009 annual letter, he wrote that a "surprising but critical fact [is] that reducing the number of [infant] deaths actually reduces population growth." "...parents choose to have enough kids to give them a high chance that several will survive to support them as they grow old. As the number of kids who survive to adulthood goes up, parents can achieve this goal without having as many children."

This may be the understanding of Bill Gates as to why parents in third world countries have lots of children but the reason could also be economic. More children are more workers who can contribute to family subsistence. They are seen as an asset in the here and now, not an investment in the future comfort of the parents. In third world countries children are seen as making poor parents rich.

I believe that Bill Gates sees humans not as a resource or holding a special place in creation. I believe he sees humans ultimately as a liability. He is a depopulationist whose father was head of Planned Parenthood. He has contributed tens of millions of dollars to groups that perform and proselytize for abortions.

If he is wrong about immunizations leading to lower populations, then his strategy of reducing infant and childhood mortality must lead to lower populations through other mechanisms resulting from overpopulation pressures. Starvation and war are other checks on overpopulation. It would be tragic indeed if his immunizations resulted in more people, more CO_2 and more suffering. In any intervention the prime directive is to first do no harm. If human beings continue to be seen as a threat to the planet because they are a source of CO_2 emissions, then the search for effective interventions will focus more on limiting human populations via inhumane measures such as sterilization and abortion. Amen

STEWARDSHIP OF TIME

"Therefore be careful how you walk, not as unwise men but as wise, making the most of your time, because the days are evil." (Eph. 5:15-16, NASB).

I was born in 1944 and now at the leading edge of the "Baby Boomers". This is a huge population bump that, if not already, will soon be drawing Social Security. What I have noticed is a tendency for many of my contemporaries including my own relatives to focus primarily on themselves. I am reminded of the words of Jesus from a portion of the Sermon on the Mount in the Gospel of Matthew. "Do not store up for yourselves treasures on earth, where moth and rust destroy, and where thieves break in and steal. But store up for yourselves treasures in heaven, where neither moth nor rust destroys, and where thieves do not break in or steal; for where your treasure is, there your heart will be also." (6:19-21, NASB).

For my generation, the time is slipping away at an ever faster pace. Many have reasonably good health, adequate finances and an uncomplicated life of leisure. They have a great deal of discretionary time every week. For me the question of what I am doing with this time is answered every morning as I journal the previous day's activities. The question for me every morning is, "Was I a good steward of the time I was given?" I am not a works righteousness type individual but do believe that Christians are called to do good works in response to God's grace and blessings. Good works are the actions that say to a loving and gracious God, "Thank you dear God; I will invest the talents you have given me. I will be a good steward of the time you have given me." "I know that there is nothing better for them than to rejoice and to do good in one's lifetime; moreover, that every man who eats and drinks sees good in all his labor–it is the gift of God." (Ecclesiastes 3:12-13, NASB).

Man was put on the earth to dress and keep the garden. That was his good works assigned to him by God. Because this work fulfilled a purpose the Creator had for man, it gave man's life meaning. There is no unemployment in the Kingdom of God and our original assignment has not changed. "We are His workmanship, created in Christ Jesus for good works, which God prepared beforehand so that we would walk in them." (Eph. 2:10, NASB).

The good works done in faith on this earth have eternal value. More and more I understand that good works redeem the time I wasted in self-indulgent and self-destructive activities. I also fully understand the sacrificial, complete and atoning death of our Lord and Savior Christ Jesus and am not saying that I need to add one more cup to His offering or His suffering. Mostly it is about awareness at this stage in my life that each day is a gift from God. It is also an impression that our good works are in giving ourselves to others in the form of a listening ear, an encouraging voice, a helping hand or an intercessory prayer.

ELVIS HAS LEFT THE BUILDING

In this week's Gospel Passage (John 4: 5-42) from the BCP lectionary, Jesus talks at length about the Spiritual realm. He talks about Himself as the water that quenches thirst permanently and brings eternal life. He also talks about doing the will of the Father as His food and the great harvest, not of crops but human souls. In the following passage however he talks about where and how God is to be worshiped.

Jesus said to her, "Woman, believe Me, an hour is coming when neither in this mountain nor in Jerusalem will you worship the Father. You worship what you do not know; we worship what we know, for salvation is from the Jews. But an hour is coming, and now is, when the true worshipers will worship the Father in spirit and truth; for such people the Father seeks to be His worshipers. God is spirit, and those who worship Him must worship in spirit and truth." (John 4:21-24, NASB).

"*Elvis has left the building!*" is a phrase that was often used by public address announcers at the end of Elvis Presley concerts to signal that there would be no more Elvis that night. There would be no more encores, he was gone and finally the audience would leave. This phrase has come to mean in a more generic sense that the end has come or put another way, there is no point in staying. When God, Who is a Spirit, is not worshiped in spirit and truth but idolatry and immorality replace spiritual worship, God will not remain.

The prophet Ezekiel in Chapter eight is taken in the spirit to the temple in Jerusalem. There he is shown idolatry and sexual immorality that was being practiced. In spite of warnings and punishment of Judah by God, the once powerful Judah was reduced almost to the point of extinction and yet they continued to descend into immorality. Abominations were taking place in the temple of God. In Chapter 10:18, God's Spirit left the temple. "Then the glory of the LORD departed from the threshold of the temple and stood over the cherubim." (NASB).

I believe there is a modern parallel to this. As in Ezekiel's day there is immorality and idolatry being practiced by a church that is turning its back on tradition and Scripture. How do we know this? We look to see what is being brought into the church. What is unholy is being called holy and blessed. It is bringing things into God's house as in the days of Ezekiel. His church is being desecrated. False doctrines and pagan living are said to be holy and blessed. And what has God done? He may dwell in His people but His spirit has left these churches. God's Shekinah glory dwelled in the temple and left the temple, gave life to the church on Pentecost and is leaving these false churches. And what is being removed? The cross of Christ is being removed because it is an offense. If these things happen in your church, then it is a sign that Elvis has left the building. Amen.

SEEKING THE LOST
PART II

I am finishing another book and this one is on Search and Rescue. There was a joy both in offering an affirmation for those who search and in the creative act of writing itself. Hopefully, the photographs used to illustrate the searches also will help tell the stories.

There is also sadness about this. It was a reliving of the disappointment of searches that became recoveries or where the individual was not found. There is an additional sadness about this for me. As we move through our lives we find ourselves reviewing chapters in our own stories. Each story is a kind of niche and we only fully realize that we have been in this niche when we are moving to the next chapter.

When I became a member of the Mountaineering Unit, my health and confidence were more robust than now. I am an ordinary person with no special search skills and what I had to offer was primarily availability, fitness, and a willingness to be led. At the same time I became involved in search and rescue work, I had also retired and had begun seminary training for Holy Orders as a Vocational Deacon.

The Spiritual niche of Deacon complimented my service as a SAR team member. Deacons are called by God to bring the needs of the people to the church and to bring the church to the people. I enjoyed incorporating some of my search stories into my sermons and remember one sermon where I held up my GPS and Satellite phone as a metaphor for not letting obstructions block communication with you and what is above you. I hope I have also brought the church to the team.

God however, was calling me to the Priesthood. It is a different Spiritual niche. It is a different chapter. At the same time he was limiting my involvement in searches because of injuries and knees that are no longer as resilient. Kneeling at the altar is almost as difficult as walking down a steep Sierra slope. A charism of a priest is pastor. Since becoming a Priest, I have taken on a different role on our team. It is a supportive role, a Barnabus role for the team leadership. They are all different from one another yet together, they are a team within a team. We have lunch on almost a weekly basis and the time together is good. It is good indeed. I was also on the team in earlier times when it was not this way.

Those of us with the gift of exhortation must use it as God has intended it. If not, an equally powerful negative side emerges and we are simply a critical person and a terrible parent to younger people. Team building is really trust building. As we serve so we become. My life has been in someone else's hands at one point or another on every search. Carrying out our assignments has helped us become more fully human. I am mourning the previous chapter as I look forward to the next chapter. Amen

HE DESTROYED THE ONE WHO HAS THE POWER OF DEATH

"The LORD God commanded the man, saying, 'From any tree of the garden you may eat freely; but from the tree of the knowledge of good and evil you shall not eat, for in the day that you eat from it you will surely die.'" (Gen. 2:16-17).

"c̲The serpent said to the woman, 'You surely will not die! For God knows (is aware) that in the day you eat from it your eyes will be opened, and d̲ you will be like God, knowing [being one with] good and evil.'" (Gen 3: 4-5).

It was not the eating of the fruit that gave them the knowledge of good and evil. Adam and Eve already knew good and gave authority over their lives to Satan through their disobedience to God and their obedience to Satan. It was the act of disobedience that allowed them to know evil. Knowing in a biblical sense means to become one with. They not only disobeyed God and obeyed Satan, they chose death over life.

That is always the choice God offers us. He offered the same choice to Israel. "I call heaven and earth to record this day against you, that I have set before you life and death, blessing and cursing: therefore choose life that both thou and Thy seed may live." (Deut. 30:19)

If we are not children of God saved by the atoning death of Jesus the Christ, we are children of Satan. We are enemies of God and children of a liar and a murderer. In our passage from Hebrews it states that Jesus through his death destroyed the one who has the power of death, that is the devil, and free those who all their lives were held in slavery by the fear of death. As Paul has stated, in Corinthians, "But Christ has indeed been raised from the dead, the first fruits of those who have fallen asleep. For since death came through a man; the resurrection of the dead comes also through a man. For as in Adam all die, so in Christ all will be made alive. But each in his own turn: Christ, the first fruits; then, when He comes, those who belong to Him. Then the end will come, when He hands over the kingdom to God the Father after He has destroyed all dominion, authority and power. For He must reign until He has put all his enemies under His feet. The last enemy to be destroyed is death. (15:20-26)

Today we, like the people in the Temple, through the witness of the Holy Spirit recognize Christ as our savior and the savior available to all nations. Today God again poses His question to us. Will we accept Christ and believe in Him? Will we chose life or reject Him and die in our sins. Lord, there is no other name whereby we are saved. With Christ as Lord we have a new master who gives us life. We reject Satan and all his works and chose new and unending life in Christ our Savior. Amen.

THEREFORE THERE IS NOW NO CONDEMNATION

In Wednesday's lectionary, the Epistle lesson is from Romans Chapter 8:1-11. There is a profound portrayal of Christ in the Prologue of St. John's Gospel. The Prologue is the finest description of Jesus the Christ using words. In Chapter Eight of Romans, St. Paul uses words to describe for me better than anywhere else who we are in Christ and our relationship to God. St. Paul's statement, "Therefore there is now no condemnation" has always been understood by commentators like Matthew Henry, John Wesley and John Darby to mean that if we are a new creature in Christ and He dwells in us then we are no longer condemned to an eternal Hell by God. I believe they are correct but I also believe there is another level that Paul intends this statement to reach. It is because Chapter eight follows the intrapersonal battle previously described in Romans chapter seven. I believe he is also talking about the voice of condemnation in our own minds. This is the daily struggle of an inner Hell addressed in Verse 33. "Who will bring any charge against those whom God has chosen?" In this case Paul is not referring to God but I believe the voice of condemnation inside our own mind.

There are times in our lives when we do or say something wrong and suddenly a voice inside our own head brings shame and humiliation immediately upon us. Have you ever actually had a hot flash and broken out in a sweat at such a time? I have.

As a Priest and a Psychologist, I know that there is a critical voice of an opportunist lying in wait to pounce upon us like a roaring lion. I believe it is the voice of one who is called the accuser of the brethren. He is also called the liar. So, even after we are a new creation we are still under attack from the false condemnation of Satan. It is he who still brings up sins we have already asked to be forgiven for and been forgiven for. It is he who tells us we are not among the elect who are cleansed by the blood of our Lord Jesus Christ. It is he who causes doubt and despair.

Does this mean that we are not also taught, led and even convicted by the Holy Spirit? Yes, that is His role in our journey of Sanctification. However, when we are accused, shamed, blamed, humiliated, it is not God the Holy Spirit doing this. He is called the comforter, the advocate and the counselor.

I believe one of the most beautiful sections from Handel's Messiah is the soprano Air, "If God Be for Us, Who Can Be against Us." Handel scored it to three verses from Romans Chapter 8 provided to him by Charles Jensen. (31) If God is for us, who can be against us? (33) Who shall lay anything to the charge of God's elect? It is God that justifies. (34) Who is he that *condemns*? It is Christ that died, yea rather, that is raised again, who is at the right hand of God, who makes intercession for us.

It is here, I think the second meaning for condemnation is understood. It is not just the eternal meaning of condemnation; it is the everyday, living the life of a Christian, understanding of what it means. This Gospel of, "God is for us" speaks life daily into a heart filled with pain, doubt and condemnation and becomes an antidote for the words of the evil one. Those words in Romans set to music by Handel still fill me with joy. Amen

SCRIPTURE: THE SEAMLESS FABRIC EMBEDDED WITH THE GOSPEL

As I was preparing my outline for Morning Prayer/Holy Eucharist tomorrow, I was reminded what a wonderful treasure the lectionary is for the church. It provides a balanced diet of Old and New Testament readings but more than that, it keeps our roots deeply planted in the Old Testament. More and more I am seeing my spiritual roots in the Old Testament.

The verse that serves as a hinge between Old and New Testament immediately precedes the Gospel Lesson.

"For the scripture saith, whosoever believeth on Him shall not be ashamed. For there is no difference between the Jew and the Greek: for the same Lord over all is rich unto all that call upon Him. For whosoever shall call upon the name of the Lord shall be saved." (Rom. 10:11-12)

This is the Gospel message for Jew and Gentile alike.

How then shall they call on him in whom they have not believed? and how shall they believe in him of whom they have not heard? and how shall they hear without a preacher? And how shall they preach, except they be sent? as it is written, How beautiful are the feet of them that preach the gospel of peace, and bring glad tidings of good things! But they have not all obeyed the gospel. For Esaias saith, Lord, who hath believed our report? So then faith cometh by hearing, and hearing by the word of God. But I say, Have they not heard? Yes verily, their sound went into all the earth, and their words unto the ends of the world. But I say, Did not Israel know? First Moses saith, I will provoke you to jealousy by them that are no people, and by a foolish nation I will anger you. But Esaias is very bold, and saith, I was found of them that sought me not; I was made manifest unto them that asked not after me. But to Israel he saith, All day long I have stretched forth my hands unto a disobedient and gainsaying people. (Romans 10:11-21)

I am amazed to say that I thought I knew and understood the Epistle Lesson and am only now beginning to understand it in the context St. Paul intended. Paul is showing that the tapestry of the Old Testament contained the Good News. He and Christ say that there is no difference between Jew and Greek. God's message of salvation was always intended for both. He was demonstrating that the Gospel had already been preached to the Jews. In this passage he quotes Old Testament Scripture no less than seven times in these passages. He is not putting a new patch on old cloth. He is uncovering for us the Gospel message imbedded in the Old Testament rejected by the Jewish people. He is using the Old Testament statements that demonstrate how the mystery of the Gospel of Jesus Christ was preexistent. It reminds me of an X-Ray of a Van Gogh's painting "Patch of Grass" that shows a portrait of a woman revealed underneath. While invisible to the naked eye, she contributes to and is a part of what we do see.

Even though there is only a remnant of the Jews, Paul understands that the Jews and Gentile Christians were a royal priesthood charged with being a blessing to others. They and we are charged with bringing glad tidings of great joy and bringing the good news of God's salvation for all people to all people that would believe and accept it.

Finally, Handel also wove Old and New Testament beautifully together with his Air for Soprano #45 "I Know My Redeemer Lives". It is a wonderful combination of verses. "I know that my Redeemer lives, and that he shall stand at the latter day upon the earth. And though worms destroy this body, yet in my flesh shall see God. (Job 19:25-26) For now is Christ risen from the dead, the first fruits of them that sleep." (I Corinthians 15:20). Amen

GRAVEYARD LAKES AREA ABOVE EDISON LAKE

THE FALSE SHEPHERDS WHO STEAL OUR FAITH

If someone asked me what my most prized possession is, I would say that it is my faith in Jesus Christ. He is the pearl of great price for which I have gone and sold all that I have. Actually, it is really not my faith at all but God's faith granted to me. If I were to lose this faith, life would have no meaning, for all that is and has meaning derives its existence and meaning from Him. I guard this faith as if my eternal life depended on it because it does depend on it.

Our faith is strengthened through prayer, Word, Sacrament and fellowship with our brothers and sisters in Christ. Our faith is nurtured and strengthened by their testimony. When we hear the Word of God faithfully preached and continue in His Word, we proceed by our own sight less. Gathering together allows us to exhort and comfort one another.

When I was going through renewal in the 1980's, I had a hunger for God's Word. I became involved in a two year Bible study series called "Crossways". The following is a comment about their goal. "Crossways International is a non-profit ministry whose goal is to foster deeper, more meaningful Christian discipleship by cultivating **biblical literacy**." I believe this series does accomplish their stated goal but there were occasional comments that caused me to ask a question that should be the litmus test of all we hear and see. "*Does this increase my faith?*" I can still remember a statement in the series, questioning what King David was really like. Scripture said that David was a man after God's own heart. Why was the Crossway author questioning the authenticity of David?

We must always remain under the authority of Scripture. It is not for us to use to Scripture to advance our own agenda or to explain Scripture in a way that justifies our own confusion or worse, unbelief. In our modern era, unbelief has become a badge of enlightened honor in the church, when it should be a cause for grave concern. In addition to the Scriptures, we are also guided by the church fathers that came to an agreement in the early councils, from whom we have inherited the Creeds. The understanding of the early church fathers is an important source and Paul warns the Galatians, "But even if we or an angel from heaven should preach a gospel other than the one we preached to you, let them be under God's curse!" (1:8). Ultimately, you are responsible for dressing and keeping the faith God has given you.

The churches today have many false shepherds who are wolves in sheep's clothing. They begin with the same question posed by the serpent in the Garden of Eden. "Did God really say that?" Whether the false shepherds are intentionally or unintentionally leading their sheep astray, they are still a tool of Satan. Do not put yourself under their spiritual authority. Do not remain in their churches. It is called the Church of Christ. Anything that diminishes Him or your faith in Him is of Satan. God the Holy Spirit is the witness to the truth in Scripture. As a believer you have the discernment and understanding of the Word of God not available to unbelievers, even if that unbeliever is a scholar or a bishop in the church. Yes, biblical literacy is important but be discerning when involved in a series and about who is leading it. Those going through renewal are those most receptive to teaching but most vulnerable also. If the teaching, sermon, interpretation, conversation does not increase your faith, it should alarm you. Amen

PRESCRIPTION STRENGTH JESUS

"The angel said to the women, "Do not be afraid; for I know that you are looking for Jesus who has been crucified. 'He is not here, for He has risen, just as He said. Come; see the place where He was lying. Go quickly and tell His disciples that He has risen from the dead'." (Matthew 28:5-7a, NASB)

I am continually amazed at those who question the reality of what we as Anglican Christians believe and proclaim in our Eucharistic Prayer every Sunday. The Priest states, "Therefore we proclaim the mystery of faith: and the Priest and People say, "Christ has died. Christ has risen. Christ will come again."

Today we celebrate both a miracle and a mystery. *The miracle and mystery of the resurrection of Jesus Christ is the centerpiece of our Christian faith*. Some have boldly denied the evidence and the fact that Christ arose from the dead. They still call themselves followers of Jesus but they are not Christians because by denying the reality of His resurrection, they deny the reality of His divinity. Their Jesus is a *"placebo Jesus"*. He is a lesser Jesus; a cheaper Jesus. Theology is not psychology and Jesus is not a placebo. Our faith in Christ is only as good as our faith that He was resurrected. If you don't believe that He was resurrected, then your Jesus was a good man and a teacher but He is not who He himself claimed to be. "Jesus answered them, "Destroy this temple, and I will raise it again in three days." They replied, "It has taken forty-six years to build this temple, and you are going to raise it in three days?" But the temple he had spoken of was His body. (John 2:19-21).

Others have tried to turn the resurrection of our Lord into a kind of subjective receptionist theology. They claim it doesn't matter if He arose from the dead. It is only important that we believe that He did. That is pure unadulterated claptrap. That is not faith at all. That is subjectivist nonsense that makes the reality of whether Christ was resurrected or not subject to the individual. Christ arose from the dead whether people believe this or not. I would call that kind of thinking "*Over the Counter Jesus*" because it has about the same efficacy as over the counter medications. Over the counter medications do not have the power to heal but they cost a lot less to obtain.

Others have attempted to offer a "*generic Jesus*". There is no generic equivalent; no generic substitute. He is original and unique. Accept no substitutes. Only He has efficacy and gives us life when we are dead. "For you died and your life is now hidden with Christ in God. When Christ, who is your life, appears, then you also will appear with H im in glory." (Colossians 3:3-4).

Yes, prescription strength Jesus is costly. It will cost you all that you have and let us remember that we must run the race to the finish. Even prescription strength medication must be taken until it is used up. If you stop taking it because you feel better, you may be risking a reinfection worse than before. However, if we remain in Christ, we will be raised as He was raised. "But Christ has indeed been raised from the dead, the first fruits of those who have fallen asleep." (1 Cor. 15:20). Amen

WHAT IS THE GOSPEL?

As someone charged with preaching the Good News of Jesus Christ, I find that it is not always as easy to articulate as I would like. If you Google "What is the Gospel?" you will get quite a variety of answers. I have selected some verses from Scripture and offer a summation following the verses. Certainly each of you has his or her favorite verse that you would add. Maybe the shortest version would be "Jesus Christ" and a more comprehensive summary would be the Nicene Creed.

"But seek ye first the kingdom of God, and his righteousness; and all these things shall be added unto you." (Matthew 6:33, NASB)

"For through the grace given to me I say to everyone among you not to think more highly of himself than he ought to think; but to think so as to have sound judgment, as God has allotted to each a measure of faith." (Romans 12:3)

"For by grace you have been saved through faith; and that not of yourselves, it is the gift of God; not as a result of works, so that no one may boast" (Ephesians 2:8-9).

"But God demonstrates His own love toward us, in that while we were yet sinners, Christ died for us." (Romans 5:8)

"But He was pierced through for our transgressions, He was crushed for our iniquities; The chastening for our well-being fell upon Him, and by His scourging we are healed." (Isaiah 53:5).

"For the wages of sin is death, but the gift of God is eternal life in Jesus Christ our Lord." (Romans 6:23)

"As far as the east is from the west, so far has He removed our transgressions from us." (Psalm 103:12)

"By this we know that we abide in Him and He in us, because He has given us of His Spirit." (1st John 4:13)

"For we are His workmanship, created in Christ Jesus for good works, which God prepared beforehand, so that we would walk in them." (Ephesians 2:10)

God by His grace has provided us with the faith to believe in and receive His Son Jesus Christ. Jesus saves us from sin, death and the devil and through the power of God The Holy Spirit given to us, the Lordship of Christ and His presence in us allows us to lead a life of love toward God and service to Christ in others.

I believe it would be a useful exercise for each of you who read this to attempt to put the Gospel in your own words. "But sanctify Christ as Lord in your hearts, always being ready to make a defense to everyone who asks you to give an account for the hope that is in you, yet with gentleness and reverence." (1st Peter 3:15) Are you ready to share the Gospel of Jesus Christ?

ALCATRAZ AND ANCHORITES

I had an opportunity to take a tour of Alcatraz this past weekend and realized that confinement is mainly a state of mind. As I walked through the cell blocks it dawned on me that prison life is a form of monasticism. There are the prisoners who take temporary vows and ones that take on permanent vows based on their past life and the strength of their convictions.

Alcatraz was a kind of monastery situated high on a rocky island surrounded by the San Francisco Bay, which is connected to the Pacific Ocean. There is a barrenness and bleakness to the main structure from which it was reputed that there was no escape. The wind was constant and the cold sea surrounding it eternally formed a moat that discouraged the prisoners from escaping. Even with the prisoners no longer there, I could sense the hopelessness and desperate effort to cling to their humanity in this place. Their names had become numbers.

I visited Mont Saint-Michel on the coast of France a few years ago and Alcatraz reminded me of it by its setting and structure. It too is an island fortress but intended to keep people out. There was a monastic community within these walls also and their warden was an abbot. They were a community of men who lived and died within the walls of

Mont St. Michael. There was however a different sense about this place. As I walked around the drafty heights I could visualize monks occupied by the task of illuminating manuscripts, prayer and the daily office. Their life was routine, confined and dedicated to poverty chastity and obedience. Their life had purpose and meaning and their vocation sought after holiness. They took on new names in accord with their station.

In Alcatraz, the solitary confinement cells 9-14 in "D" Block were considered the harshest living conditions for those who refused to obey the rules of the order of prisoners. Their cells were carved out of the wall of the prison which forms the back of their cell. They were only allowed out of their cells for a weekly shower. Their vows were similar to the monks but imposed on them for a similar reason by the prison warden. The rules are for conversion of manners also. Those in solitary confinement lived the contemplative life with opportunity for visions. Robert "Birdman of Alcatraz" Stroud was probably the most famous of the unrepentant residents of D Block.

Anchorites lived in a cell formed from part of a monastery wall. The door to the cell was permanently sealed with bricks and they lived in this cell until they died. Their bodily waste was removed by a chamber pot and they were brought food and fed though a small opening in a common wall. My wife and I visited a church in Ireland that had a cell in the sanctuary wall for an anchorite. St. Julian of Norwich was an anchoress in the medieval period that led a contemplative life and experienced visions. An anchorite was considered a source of spiritual advice and counsel to abbots.

Some monastics eventually leave the order because they find the life too limiting. Some prisoners return because they find freedom too confining. Each of us lives much of our daily life in a cell of similar dimensions without walls, sometimes with partitions. Are you in prison or are you free? "To know You is eternal life and to serve You is perfect freedom." (Book of Common Prayer, from "A Collect for Peace" p. 99). Amen

THE CHURCH OF FRESNO

I seem to live a life of contrasts. Last weekend we were in San Francisco for the wedding of our youngest son. It is a beautiful city with world class views, top drawer hotels and great places to dine. The air is good in this white collar town but this is not about San Francisco.

This is my 20th year in Fresno, a city of half a million people. When I first arrived from the Midwest, two things were immediately apparent. Most of the homes had burglar alarms and graffiti was pervasive. Things seemed to turn around when an ecumenical group of clergy who named themselves, "The No Name Fellowship" gathered together to regularly pray for Fresno. There is also an annual clergy prayer summit. Some clergy even took up residence in some of the worst areas in the city. In the year 2000 Fresno was named an "All American City." Fresno is a city of faith. When so much is said about the post Christian society and godless government, Fresno is a city of prayer. Fresno's clergy and parishioners have gathered together regularly to pray for their city. It is a church city. It is the Church of Fresno.

I was at the annual memorial ceremony for fallen peace officers in Courthouse Park today. As a civilian member of our

Fresno County Sheriff's Search and Rescue Team, our twenty six blaze orange shirts stood out against the dress uniforms of other departments around the state of California. It was a small town event in a large California city.

It began with a helicopter fly over and a drum and bagpipe group that preceded the state and national flags. Our hands were on our hearts as the flags went by. A school choir sang the National Anthem, an Episcopal Hymn, "Author of Majesty, Love and Grace" and the "Battle Hymn of the Republic". There were also two solos by peace officers, "To Make You Feel My Love" and "Believe". Two judges gave brief speeches honoring the families followed by the Roll Call of Fallen Officers. There was a prayer from the chaplain for the Sheriff's Department who concluded with, "…. in the name of Jesus Christ". Then "Amazing Grace", a 21 gun salute and "Taps". All of the participants, families and guests were invited to a buffet following the event.

This was not really a Memorial Ceremony. It was more of a church service, in the center of a city in the center of California. Our Mayor, Police Chief, and County Sheriff are Christians. They don't make a big show of it but they don't hide it either. Fresno is a city that is not ashamed of Christ. It is diverse as any California city but the churches here are attended by a great many of its citizens and respected by most of those who don't attend.

This is where a mix of agrarian, blue collar and white collar Christianity still thrives alongside of each other and cynicism, postmodernism, and relativism have not taken root. Our Sikh volunteer officer Nick was at my right shoulder with his hand over his heart as our flag went by and his head was bowed as we prayed. Fresno is a place of compassion, mercy and hope. May God continue to bless His Church of Fresno. Amen

NAPS

"For He gives to His beloved even in his sleep." (Psalm 127:2b)

For some reason, the need to sleep is viewed by many as a weakness. My grandchildren resist sleep until they are overtaken by it. The diagnosis for cranky children is that they are tired and the prescription is that they need a nap. My late father used to deny that he had fallen asleep reading the paper. "I was only resting my eyes."

I am here to confess that in addition to 8 hours of sleep at night, I also take naps almost daily. There, I've said it and if you think I am weak then so be it. Those who claim that they never nap like to rub it in with a large dose of guilt. They exclaim, "I could never find the time to nap. My day is so busy." I also arise at 4am in the morning and retire at 8pm in the evening. It has been this way for the last twenty five years or so. Friends and relatives so enjoy saying, "Oh, it's 8pm, Dale must simply be exhausted, wink, wink."

When I tell others that I take naps and look forward to them, I get looks of puzzlement or pity or discomfort like I had just admitted to watching professional wrestling on a regular basis. These same people tell me that they only sleep about 5 or 6 hours a night and never nap. Well, I guess they are real grownups and don't need that much sleep.

My naps tend to be of two kinds. The *hard* naps are about 45 minutes to an hour. These are the naps I awaken from and wonder what day it is. Someone who is closely related to me but will remain nameless has been known to take 3-4 hour naps on occasion. She rarely naps intentionally. My favorite nap is on Sunday afternoon following a sermon at two services. I've earned that nap and there is absolutely no prior guilt. (Some of our parishioners have chosen to nap during my sermons).

There is also a *short* nap that can be of 10-15 minutes duration. It is unbelievable how restorative these short naps can be. As an ultrarunner, I used to train a lot on the trails of Yosemite. During the drive home, the endorphins would combine with the fatigue to gradually overpower my sense of alertness. I could feel myself falling asleep. The Wawona Store parking lot was my short nap midpoint refuge. Following a mere 15 minute nap, the 64 miles back to Fresno was easy.

Here is the point of my confession without contrition. Go ahead and take a nap and by His authority committed to me, I absolve you of your guilt.

"Sweet sleep that knits the ravell'd sleeves of care" (Macbeth)

WHAT IS OUR DAILY BREAD?

In our Lectionary Gospel lesson for Wednesday in the third week of Easter Christ states, "I am the bread of life; he who comes to Me will not hunger, and he who believes in Me will never thirst." (John 6:35, NASB) "Your forefathers ate the manna in the desert, yet they died. But here is the bread that comes down from heaven, which a man may eat and not die. I am the living bread that came down from heaven. If anyone eats of this bread, he will live forever. This bread is my flesh, which I will give for the life of the world." (John 6:49-51)

What is our daily bread? In Luther's catechism speaking on our Lord's Prayer, Luther defines it thus:

"*What is meant by daily bread?*–Answer. <u>Everything that belongs to the support and wants of the body</u>, such as meat, drink, clothing, shoes, house, homestead, field, cattle, money, goods, a pious spouse, pious children, pious servants, pious and faithful magistrates, good government, good weather, peace, health, discipline, honor, good friends, faithful neighbors and the like."

I believe it is here that Luther misunderstands what Jesus is teaching us in the Lord's Prayer by understanding our daily bread as support for the body. That is the kingdom of this world. Luther is interpreting our daily bread in the sense of the Old Testament wilderness experience of the manna God provided daily for sustenance for the Israelites. That is not however what Christ is referring to.

In Matthew Chapter 6, Christ provides both His prayer and the context for understanding our daily bread. Following His presentation of the prayer (6:9-13), He then discusses the unnecessary and material concerns of the world in verses 19-32. "So, do not worry, saying, 'What shall we eat?' or 'What shall we drink?' or 'What shall we wear?' For the pagans run after all these things, and your heavenly Father knows that you need them. These are the material concerns that Luther incorrectly refers to as our daily bread. In verse 6:33 Christ states, "But seek first his kingdom and his righteousness, and all these things will be given to you as well." The daily bread Christ is referring to is the daily bread required for sustenance in the Kingdom of God. He is referring to Himself.

"Just as the living Father sent Me and I live because of the Father, so the one who feeds on Me will live because of Me. This is the bread that came down from heaven. Your forefathers ate manna and died, but he who feeds on this bread will live forever." (John 6:57-58).

My brothers and sisters, there is no purer Gospel than this. Christ has brought us back into the Garden of Eden. We again may partake of the tree of life. He continues to feed His people the church with His body and blood and has done so for two thousand years. In the Eucharist, we are given the bread with these words spoken, "The body of Christ; the bread of heaven." When we are given the chalice, we are told, "The blood of Christ; the cup of salvation." In Him we have eternal life and in Him we are more than conquerors. Just as Yahweh provided daily manna in the wilderness to the Israelites, Christ offers himself as our bread daily in the Kingdom of God. Lord, give us this day our daily bread. Amen

GOD'S OMNIPRESENCE

"Where can I go from Your Spirit? Or where can I flee from Your presence? If I ascend to heaven, You are there; If I make my bed in Sheol, behold, You are there. If I take the wings of the dawn, If I dwell in the remotest part of the sea, Even there Your hand will lead me, And Your right hand will lay hold of me." (Psalm 139:7-10, NASB)

A mysterious quality of God is His omnipresence and it is of great comfort to me as I better understand *how* God is ever present. While His presence and involvement in our lives is not always evident at the time, upon reflection we can see in the rear view mirror of faith how God was orchestrating a host of seemingly unrelated events toward an obtained goal we may not have even strived for.

Increasingly, I see the manna laid daily before me. It is not difficult to see the incremental aspect to professional progress. Look at any curriculum vitae and you can see how the educational and experiential history is directed toward a particular career. It is also not difficult to see the incremental aspect of training to run a marathon. No runner attempts a marathon without the perfunctory runs at shorter distances. It is the career counselor or coach who can see the goal of a career or a marathon more clearly than the individual caught up in the activities of daily living. God the Holy Spirit is our coach and counselor.

Being aware of God's omnipresence is knowing that God is in it with us and that He is willing to share His perspective with us. He has the long view in mind; the eternal view. He is underneath all of those things we do; all of those things that happen to us. So much of what we are doing in a life committed to the will of God requires reflection on how the activities are leading in a particular direction or toward a particular goal. God is in this. God is orchestrating this for us.

Prophesy is as much about a better understanding what has gone before as it is about the future. I now know that God always was and is present in my life and this knowledge has positively reconstructed negative memories and provided consolations. It also makes suffering in the present tolerable and provides meaning for this life lived in a world hell bent on destroying itself.

God is a master builder. Reexamine what you have done over the last five years. Are there incremental aspects, seemingly unrelated that when assembled, are a goal accomplished that you had not even considered? As an example of this, I had always wanted to write a book and knew that there was a book inside of me. One day I was reviewing many of the blog articles I had written over the last two years and realized that if combined, they would constitute a book. Additionally, they factored into two groupings. They had to do with comfort and exhortation. What a revelation that was for me in and of itself!

There is a famous story about a single set of footprints on a beach. The individual complains that God is not with her only to be told by God that the single set of footprints is when He had carried the individual. "...and lo, I am with you always, even to the end of the age." (Matthew 28:20b).

A PRAYER OF PETITION

Lord Jesus come into my heart. Come into my life. Give me Your precious life. Bring the Father with You. Bring the Spirit with You.

Bring Your peace that I may cast my cares upon You. Bring Your life that I may never thirst again. Bring Your heart so my thoughts may be pure before You. Bring the oil of gladness and the balm of Gilead too. Bring Your wisdom that I may avoid wrong actions. Share Your innocence to cleanse my intentions. Bring Your thoughts that my mind will be transformed. Lend Your will that mine may be the same.

Bring Your joy that my sadness will depart from me. Bring Your love that I may see You in others. Bring Your humility that my pride will fall away. Bring Your compassion that I will forget about myself. Bring Your faith that mountains will be removed. Bring Your hope to run the race before me.

Bring Your garments that I may be clothed in righteousness. Bring Your brokenness that I may be made whole. Amen

WITHOUT FAITH WORKS IS DEAD

You are probably thinking, Fr. Dale, you must have meant to say, "Even so faith, if it has no works, is dead, being by itself." (James 2:17, NASB) Well, I did not intend to say that but it is true also.

I am actually more concerned that the contemporary church is replete with works but the works are devoid of faith. "And without faith it is impossible to please Him, for he who comes to God must believe that He is and that He is a rewarder of those who seek Him." (Hebrews 11:6, NASB).

Faith requires an object and for Christians, this is Jesus the Christ. Historic heresies are continually reintroduced into the church and are fashionable again today. The central issue of Christian faith hinges on Christ, who for Christians is the object of and center of that faith. Many heresies attempt to dehumanize Him on one side and strip Him of His divinity on the other. He came to reveal the Father and if we lose sight of Him, we lose sight of the Father also.

There is one work in particular that concerns me and that work is *Justice*. "What should we say, then? That the gentiles, although they were not looking for saving justice, found it, and this was the saving justice that comes of faith; while Israel, looking for saving justice by law-keeping, did not succeed in fulfilling the Law. And why is this? Because they were trying to find it in actions and not in faith, and so they stumbled over the stumbling-stone-"(Romans 9:30-32 NJB)

If our faith is not connected to Christ, we do not even understand justice. Justice is considered one of the four cardinal virtues of the church. Justice does not begin with what we believe our rights are. It begins with what the rights of God are and what God has declared what we deserve. "For the wages of sin is death; but the gift of God is eternal life through Jesus Christ our Lord." (Romans 6:23). God has determined that we deserve damnation in Hell for eternity. That is where justice begins for us and it is difficult to hear. A grace disconnected from this understanding of justice does not appreciate the mercy of God nor does it comprehend the atoning work of our Lord Jesus Christ.

Justice first and foremost respects the rights of God; of what He is worthy to receive because He is God. We are to love Him before our neighbor or ourselves. Justice centered only on the rights of humans becomes relative, situational and confused.

"Many will say to me in that day, 'Lord, Lord, have we not prophesied in Thy name? And in Thy name have cast out devils? And in Thy name done many wonderful works?' And then will I profess unto them, 'I never knew you: depart from Me, ye that work iniquity.'" (Matthew 7:22-23, NASB). Amen.

HELL

"We must not ask where hell is, but how we are to escape it" St. Chrysostom."

The historic view of the major denominations is that Hell is the place of eternal torment. This position is softening and The Church of England Commission on Doctrine (1995) embraced an Annihilationist view. This is the foot in the door for eventual Universalism. The Book Of Common Prayer (1979) seems to have already adopted the Annihilationist view. "By hell, we mean eternal death in our rejection of God." (p.862)

In St. Paul's 2nd letter to the Church in Corinth (Chapter 12), he stated that fourteen years earlier, he was given a glimpse of heaven. It had such a lasting effect on him, he noted in his letter to the Philippian Church (Chapter 1), that he wanted to depart and be with Christ.

I gave my life to Christ when I was eight years old and remember asking God when I was about twelve to take me to heaven then if I would ever fall away. There was also a period of many years where I had fallen away and rejected Christ. I know that if I had died at that time, I would have gone to Hell. I am not an advocate of "once saved always saved".

I think Christians who fall away do so gradually. Like an anorexic, they are unaware that they are spiritually starving while other can see it. When I came back to Christ and was baptized as an adult, I had a thirst for scripture like a man rescued from the desert has a thirst for water. After receiving a new Thompson Chain Link Reference Bible (KJV) for my Baptism, I had the opportunity to study God's Word with zeal.

I had been fascinated by the book of Revelation since childhood. When I was a child, it was fearful reading. All of a sudden I had this idea that it would be me that would make sense of Revelation. I would decode the deeper mysteries. As I began to study Revelation it began to dawn on me that all of Revelation had already come to pass. All those who would go to Heaven were already there.

There is a qualitative difference between gradually pulling away from God and a sudden awareness that there is permanent gulf between me and God with no hope of crossing the chasm. I cannot describe how despondent, filled with despair, hopeless and alone I was at that moment. I was in Hell.

During the next few days, I thought about people like Billy Graham and my spiritual mentor Jim Bolling. Surely God would not allow people like that to be in Hell? My dear Christian mother was still living. I clung to John 3:16 for dear life. Eventually the passage, "In My Father's house are many dwelling places; if it were not so, I would have told you; for I go to prepare a place for you." (John 14:2, NASB) offered me comfort where there was none previously. And then the final passages from Romans 8 came to mind. "For I am convinced that neither death, nor life, nor angels, nor principalities, nor things present, nor things to come, nor powers, nor height, nor depth, nor any other created thing, will be able to separate us from the love of God, which is in Christ Jesus our Lord." (NASB). Like St. Paul's glimpse of Heaven, God had given me a glimpse of what Hell was like. Hell is real and I don't want to go there.

"And they that have done good shall go into life everlasting; and they that have done evil into everlasting fire." (From the Creed of St. Athanasius).

A PRAYER OF INTERCESSION: NATURAL DISASTERS

Lord watch over those who have survived. Comfort the grieving. Orient the lost and confused. Placate the angry and give peace to the frightened. Provide meaning and purpose for the suffering that it may be redemptive and not destructive. May they reach out to others that share a common bond and remember those things that allow them to continue and transcend their current station. Give new roots to the uprooted. Restore the workplace and the economy for the sake of their dignity and independence. Extend Your mercy and send consolations to the broken and broken hearted.

Protect those who search and administer help, from injury, despair and exhaustion. Give wisdom and courage to those who administer relief. Let them not be overwhelmed. Let them receive mercy as they extend mercy.

Knit together those of us who watch or hear from a distance, with those who weep. Help us to lend our prayers and share our goods. Let us not be overcome, walk by or look away. Show us how to help. May we see You in them and shed tears for those no longer able to do so. Lord our sorrow for them runs so deep, we struggle to breathe.

Give eternal peace and rest to those who perished. May they remain with You forever and may they remain with us, hidden and protected in the innermost sanctuary of our hearts. May we be united in heavenly communion with them here and be reunited with them when we depart to be with You in Your Heavenly Kingdom. Amen

WHY I GOT OFF FACEBOOK

Unless you are a hermit, friends are a big part of your life. When I initially joined Facebook, I had about 10 friends there. Over time more people wanted to be my friend. One person who I didn't know wanted to befriend me and was upset that I turned him down. Is Facebook a place to make friends or meet friends or both? I was also bothered by people who did not have a photograph of themselves for their avatar. Some had none while others used a group or pets.

As time went on, more people asked to be my friend. Some were people who wanted to make a professional relationship a personal one. I felt like personal boundaries were being crossed. In fact the idea of *intrusion* began to come up more and more. I was *invited* to join causes, play games or buy farm animals. There is a kind of social coercion to this similar to being invited to a party by a friend only to find that it is for Amway.

There was another issue that was eating away at me. I was continually being exposed to the remarks of friends of friends and some of these remarks were downright uncivil. It was like being at a stop light alongside of a car with open windows blasting Hyper Bass Gansta Rap. There are also shorthand codes like LOL or ROFL or OMG. I would rather learn Greek.

People were using Facebook to private mail me. Well, why not just email me? There is one less step. People were asking me to conduct business on Facebook including sending attachments. Again, Outlook is vastly superior.

Part of this is that while I am gregarious, I am also an introvert. When I went over 100 friends, I said to myself, "This seems like a lot of people." Of the 100, I think I only asked about 5 people to be my friends. How did this get so out of control? It was like someone living in Fresno finding himself on Interstate 5 in Los Angeles during rush hour where it is always rush hour.

There is something virtual and unreal about Facebook relationships. Even with a telephone, there is a sensual quality about the presence of another person. There is a kind of parallel play on Facebook too. Are people talking to one another or alongside of one another? The activities of daily living are shared as if it mattered that Joe went to the store. I don't even write the mundane things in my personal journal that people post to Facebook.

There is "look at me" narcissism to Facebook that was growing in me too. I was sharing more information than I should and sharing more often than I should. There was no corrective feedback about this that would have come from a friend in a conversation over a shared meal. There was a kind of good dying to leaving Facebook.

"Abstinence is easier than perfect moderation." Aristotle

LAKE MARY SKI LOOP MAMMOTH LAKES AREA

THE FINAL STAGE OF LIFE

"I know what it is to be in need, and I know what it is to have plenty. I have learned the secret of being content in any and every situation, whether well fed or hungry, whether living in plenty or in want." (Philippians 4:12, NASB).

I have entered what the developmental psychologist Erik Erikson referred to as the eighth and final stage of life. It is called Ego Integrity versus despair. Each stage of development for Erikson holds a challenge that must be mastered.

What is not generally considered is that old age does not present a singular final stage task. It requires the integration of all the tasks of the previous stages and the same questions answered at previous stages demand different answers in the final stage. Do I trust those around me? Am I a good person? Who am I? The answer to who I am as an adolescent is different than the answer to who I am as an older adult. I am no longer defined by professional affiliations and credentials. Many personal bests are behind me but I have found that there is a creative surge less limited by distractions, and informed by experiences. What I have to give is no longer material.

What saddens me is that many of my lifelong friends have stopped looking forward with optimism. There is an unnecessary cynicism, mistrust and guardedness. There is resentment about how things turned out. They have not made the good transition to old age. In some cases their vocations defined who they had become. Once retired, they began to shrink. It is not that they took a wrong turn as much as they stopped moving altogether. They stopped being engaged and initiating. They stopped being a grown up and became a victim.

They became hyperreflective and lost the battle of intimacy won in a previous stage. Their self-worth was based on their sense of productivity and the myth of personal power. Their perspective did not successfully expand to embrace the importance of a good word spoken at the precise time. They never came to understand the universe changing prayer of intercession. They are drawing down their account with no more deposits. Their depression is self-induced and fed with predictive certainty.

It does not have to be this way. Things can still be turned around. The final stage of life can be one of contentment. Yes, there is a loss of power, dignity, autonomy and productivity but as John the Baptist said, "He must increase but I must decrease" (John 3:30, NASB). For the Christian, loss is gain and dying is gaining eternal life. This life is not about us. It never was and never will be. Our final self; the finished product is Jesus Christ.

"I can do all things through Him who strengthens me."(Philippians 4:13, NASB)

SEX DRUGS AND ROCK AND ROLL: CHOOSING DEATH

Chorus
Sex and drugs and rock and roll
Is all my brain and body need.
Sex and drugs and rock and roll
Are very good indeed. (Ian Dury 1977)

"But for the cowardly, the faithless, the vile, the murderers, those who commit sexual immorality, those who use drugs and cast spells, the idolaters and all liars—their share will be in the lake that burns with fire and sulfur. This is the second death." (Rev. 21:8, Common English Bible).

The late Ian Dury's lyrics were not a 1970's anthem signaling a new era. The lyrics were a summative mantra portraying a decline that had already become mainstream in the 1960's. The era of the 1960's was a turning point for Western Society and I was very much a part of it.

Birth control pills were drugs that allowed for sex without pregnancy and were introduced in 1960. At that time sexually transmitted diseases were not as rampant or as potentially deadly. It was called "Free Love" but it was really uncommitted serial sexual encounters. The late Billy Preston coined the phrase, "If you can't be with the one you love, love the one you're with" and it later became the title of a song by Stephen Stills (1970). We knew what it meant.

If Charles Wesley conveyed faith, service and doctrine through his hymns, the Beatles, "Satan's Jesters" the Rolling Stones, and later groups like Guns and Roses breathed new life into an "old immorality". It was anti-government, disrespect for authority, anarchistic, hedonistic and narcissistic. Heavy Metal Groups followed with names like Megadeath and Black Sabbath and spewed nihilist notions of their own. I worked Grateful Dead concerts in Wisconsin as a mental health counselor and saw firsthand the drug induced hell they brought with them. Drugs are not just the cause of so much sorrow and death. Drugs are a symptom of a life devoid of meaning and purpose seeking respite from a living hell through self-medication. There is also the inestimable legacy of brain damaged and aborted children.

"I call heaven and earth to witness against you today, that I have set before you life and death, the blessing and the curse. So choose life in order that you may live, you and your descendants." (Deuteronomy 30:19).

My generation chose death and is rightfully looked at with condescension and contempt by succeeding generations. As my cohort finds itself in the final developmental stage moving toward the death they so avidly courted and embraced during their lives, they mistakenly think that recycling and driving a Prius will undo the damage they have inflicted on the generations that follow and sooth the guilt they attempt to deny.

The theme song for my generation is "Sex, Drugs and Rock and Roll". The fitting recessional hymn could be "Is That All There Is?" It was also a late 1960's song by Peggy Lee. We were vain and conceited and we took God for granted. I hope and pray that those who follow us will find meaning and purpose in Jesus The Christ. I ask that God and they would forgive us. As we approach the Season of Pentecost may God the Holy Spirit fall upon us afresh, quicken our mortal bodies and renew our strength. Amen

THE IN BETWEEN TIMES: DO NOT LEAVE US COMFORTLESS

A portion of our Collect for the Seventh Sunday of Easter states, "Do not leave us comfortless, but send us your Holy Spirit". We are at an important in between place in the church year. We are awaiting comfort and empowerment. Christ ascended into Heaven forty days after Easter. Ascension Day is one of the seven Principal Feast Days in the church year and was celebrated last Thursday. Next Sunday is another of the seven Principal Feast Days. It is the Day of Pentecost where the Holy Spirit descends on the Apostles and the Church is born, empowered to proclaim the Good News of Jesus Christ. Until this point, the Apostles were spending a good deal of time behind a locked door in the upper room. They were obediently waiting but while they waited, there was no boldness, only fear. They had seen their resurrected Lord for forty days and then He ascended to Heaven. Christ told the Apostles to wait a few days in Jerusalem for empowerment by the Holy Spirit. He said they would receive a "baptism". This period of waiting did amount to a matter of days and this Sunday would be day three of ten. The in between time from Christ's Ascension to Pentecost was ten days.

There is a repeated cycle of joy and sadness for the Apostles with the <u>in between</u> waiting times. In the story of Lazarus, Christ's friends were happy to see Him but sad that He had not come sooner. While they awaited His arrival, their brother Lazarus died.

After the Israelites fled Egypt, they spent forty years wandering in the wilderness before they crossed the Jordan River into the Promised Land. There is a purpose to the <u>in between</u> times. It is waiting on the Spirit of God to fall upon us afresh. It is to learn patience and obedience. It is to seek the will of God.

How much of your life has taken place in the <u>in between times</u>? How often has a situation seemed to drag on with no resolution? How about the letter from the insurance company? How about that job you applied for? Why haven't you heard anything yet? What about the diagnosis? When will the doctor's office call you about it? Have you prayed about it? Have you prayed and prayed about it and not received an answer? Have you finally come to a place where you said, "Not my will Lord but Your will be done."

Christ was awaiting His arrest in the Garden of Gethsemane and wanted God to remove the sentence of death from Him. It was a terrible <u>in between time</u> for Him. It was the time between His arrest and His crucifixion. It is so hard to say to God, "Thy will be done".

The church itself also called the bride of Christ is in the <u>in between times</u> awaiting the return of the bridegroom. The church is called to be in the world and not of it. This view shapes the church's response to this same culture.

We are not left comfortless during these <u>in between</u> times. Christ was born, Christ died and Christ will come again. The Holy Spirit is here to comfort us. He is here and even called the comforter and the counselor. He is the one called alongside as the advocate. He is that still small voice offering exhortation, encouragement and empowerment. Listen to Him. Listen to Him in the silences between the background noises. He has much to tell you. Amen.

MY TESTIMONY

"Today I have given you the choice between life and death, between blessings and curses. Now I call on heaven and earth to witness the choice you make. Oh, that you would choose life, so that you and your descendants might live!" (Deuteronomy 30:19, NLT).

I was given a Halley's Bible Handbook for High School Graduation at the Baptist Church I had attended since childhood. It was also a graduation of sorts from church also for the next twenty years. It was the usual time of life for questioning things in general and it was a time when "God is dead" was the mantra of the professors at my University. The decade of the 60's was horrible in general and worse for young men in particular. While some relish reminiscing, I think about the instability of life following the previous quiescent decade. Leaders such as President Kennedy, Martin Luther King and Robert Kennedy were assassinated in what seemed like an outbreak of unending anarchy. I was drafted into the Army out of the University my senior year because my grade point average did not meet the criteria for the local draft board. During my two years of service I went from someone with a drinking problem to someone with a serious drinking problem. I remember taking money from a donation canister in a store to buy alcohol. What had I become?

For the next sixteen years I was engaged in the process of killing myself on the installment plan. Addiction to alcohol and cigarettes was only part of a self-defeating and self-destructive lifestyle. I had a rage inside me coupled with a fear that paralyzed personal growth and hurt those around me. I desperately sought peace and found alcohol to be a dependable source. It was a however a deal with the devil. Mornings became more and more difficult. I had panic attacks so severe, I would have to pull off the road in the tractor trailer hauling heavy equipment and sit until the fear passed.

I planned my life around alcohol and always made sure there was enough around to get the job done. While I never drank at work, I had a string of jobs over the years where I fouled my own nest over time. I was a husband and a father but emotionally unavailable to my wife and sons except in a harsh and punitive sense. I believe at this time of my life, I was capable of any act and fortunately God didn't allow opportunities to present themselves.

God in His grace can even reach into the heart of the active unrepentant addict. I signed up for a sixteen week adult bible study with my wife as an act of appeasement, at the local Lutheran Church. After the first night I remember banging my fist on the steering wheel and saying that I wasn't going back. During that sixteen weeks, God the Holy Spirit courted me and won me back. I had given my life to Christ as an eight year old in Sunday school. The crucial question for me was the same one Christ posed to Peter. "Who do you say that I am?" To see Christ as God opened the door for my return. I began attending bible class between services and enjoyed the experience immensely. Jim B., the president of the congregation, became my spiritual mentor. He answered my many questions and became a father to me. He has passed on now but his biological son became a pastor and his adoptive son became a priest. It is part of a fitting eulogy for a godly man. He is only the first of many good men and women God placed by my side.

God's will is not initially heavy but the cumulative effect is a rod of iron. I gradually became aware, following my baptism, that there was no turning back. I remember the thought that came to me before I walked down the aisle for my baptism. "You are throwing your life away for this Jesus". The statement was true but the life I was throwing away wasn't worth living. I was now another ambassador of God's Kingdom and as an ambassador; it was not fitting for me to be a drunk or a smoker. At one point in my life, I had such severe indigestion from drinking that I put baking soda in my wine to avoid the acid stomach. I actually believed the lie that I would die if I quit drinking. I prayed about this and was delivered from the need to drink. I was trustworThy again. I had to pray for two more years to get the desire to quit smoking and when I quit on January 10th 1983, I never smoked again. I believe there can be conversion from addiction also.

There can be an enormous release of pent up power in a recovering individual. I will state unequivocally, that God chose me as He chose so many others to demonstrate His power. <u>I am an ordinary man</u> with a limited amount of physical and intellectual aptitude. For the next ten years God began to release His creative and life giving power in my life. I went back to school and finished my Ph.D. at Marquette University in Educational Psychology. On my first day of classes at Marquette (a Jesuit University) I looked up to see a crucifix on the wall. It seemed so right to me. I was an average student in high school and an honor student in graduate school. I also became a licensed Psychologist and School Psychologist. During this time I also designed and built a home and ran my first marathon. Running became my replacement behavior for smoking. At one point my weight, blood pressure and cholesterol were in the extreme range and in need of medical intervention. Running and a change of diet solved another aspect of a self-destructive life. "I can do all things through Christ which strengthens me." (Philippians 4:13, KJV)

There was also unexpected collateral damage. My marriage of more than 20 years was falling apart. We fought more than ever. We were two decent people who now only seemed to bring out the worst in each other. The rancor was difficult for our sons. We agreed that I would take a tenure track teaching position in California at a Mennonite Brethren University and the family would join me the following year after my oldest son had graduated from high school. It did not come to pass and we agreed to a Pro Se divorce. My university spent nearly a year investigating the circumstances. It was a difficult and lonely time. The same week in December of 1993 our divorce was finalized and the university agreed to allow me to stay on. Once again, God provided a saintly mentor Dr. Bob W., who I worked with for over eight years. His passing is mourned by hundreds of former students that he both taught and shepherded.

After seventeen years of teaching and being a school psychologist, I was no longer able to convince myself that was what God had intended as my final career. As a program director, I was able to both teach and counsel the students in the counseling and school psychology programs. Part of our evaluation was our participation in our church and I could see that increasing year by year with a declining passion for teaching and the academic life.

In the meantime, I walked into church one Sunday thinking that I would never meet a woman there who could be my wife. God's humor is manifested at times like this. As I was sitting down in the pew, I looked across the aisle to my right and in front of me. There was a woman sitting there that was the most handsome woman I have ever seen. She had the most beautiful gray hair and a youthful face that betrayed the gray hair. Sharon was visiting with a friend who was a parishioner there. I said to myself, "I will meet this woman no matter what it takes". I had coffee with her at a small local grill on Monday and knew within the next week that we would be married. She also had been divorced about three years. Between us we have four sons. We were married at the foot of Bridalveil Falls in Yosemite in 1996.

While I was still teaching at the university, I began taking classes in Anglican Studies at the Mennonite Brethren Biblical Seminary on the campus of Fresno Pacific University where I taught. I loved the theology and history of Anglicanism and began to sense that God was calling me to holy orders. Unfortunately for me the members of the Commission on Ministry decided after meeting with me that I needed more time to discern my call. This was a polite way of saying that my ego had metastasized and needed a two year course of rejection therapy. I was more humble at my next retreat and had retired as emeritus from Fresno Pacific University.

There remained questions about whether I was being called to the Deaconate or the Priesthood and following a year working as a vocational Deacon, I met with Bishop Schofield to say that I really thought God was calling me to the Priesthood. His response was, "What took you so long"? After a year of additional training and experience, I was ordained a Priest on the Feast Day of St. Gregory the Great, March 12th 2010. It is where God wanted me to be all along but it took me until age 65 to be prepared for this calling.

God has called me above all to comfort others with the comfort that I have been comforted with. "Blessed be the God and Father of our Lord Jesus Christ, the Father of mercies and God of all comfort, who comforts us in our entire affliction so that we will be able to comfort those who are in any affliction with the comfort with which we ourselves are comforted by God." (2 Cor. 1:3-4). I know others who have been prodigals but they have had enormous gifts. What makes my testimony unique is that I am ordinary. If God can accomplish this with me then a similar life dedicated and submitted to God can also demonstrate the Glory of God. "But you are a chosen race, a royal priesthood, a holy nation, a people for God's own possession, so that you may proclaim the excellences of Him who has called you out of darkness into His marvelous light." (1 Peter 2:9). My personal prayer for those who read this would be that they would have hope that Christ could, like Lazarus also raise them from a self-destructive life. Amen

EVELYN UNDERHILL: MYSTIC

"For he who comes to God must believe that He is and that He is a rewarder of those who seek Him." (Hebrews 11:6b, NASB)

June 15th is the Anglican Feast Day of Evelyn Underhill (1875-1941). Perhaps the most salient comment about her in "Lesser Feasts and Fasts" is, "Evelyn Underhill's most valuable contribution to spiritual literature must surely be her conviction that the mystical life is not only open to a saintly few, but to anyone who cares to nurture it…"

Mysticism is an important ingredient in the Prescription Strength Church. I find it extraordinary that a woman from the lay order of the church would instruct clergy in the Church of England in her day. By what authority did she speak? We know. She, like other mystics had an insatiable hunger for God and understood sanctification as a developmental process. Like the Kingdom of God however, it is an upside down developmental process. We don't "Self Actualize" (Maslow) or "Individualize" (Jung).

"Underhill's research indicates that there two distinct thrusts or directions to the full mystic consciousness. One is the increasing consciousness or vision of God; the other is the inner transmutation of the personality, the rebuilding or the restructuring of the self on an inward and deeply all pervasive level. Neither thrust can be accomplished without the complete transcendence of the small ego-centric self" (<u>Ordinary People as Monks and Mystics</u> Marsha Sinetar, 1986).

Spiritual development requires an ongoing surrender and submission to God. For the mystic, there is a restlessness that cannot find rest until they find rest in God. The mystic divests himself of his own identity through ongoing conversion to Christ who is his new and authentic identity. This is different than the psychotic who cannot give up an identity that he never had to begin with.

She saw mysticism as a normal part of the Christian Church. Mysticism is not ethereal; it is the meat and potatoes of intentional spiritual development. Her lifelong attraction to the Roman Catholic Church as a repository of mystery and mysticism opposed a more rationalist and enlightened Anglican heritage that diminished the miraculous and iconography. The sensual avenues of God's presence had become sidewalks.

Benedict Groeschel has an excellent description of Spiritual Development toward the mystical life in his book "Spiritual Passages: The Psychology of Spiritual Development" (1993) that is in basic agreement with Underhill's spiritual developmental stages. His stages are Purgative, Illuminative, and Unitive. In the Unitive stage there is a loss of all defenses (again this is different than the psychotic who also is undefended). This final stage is quite different for the Christian than the Nirvana of a Buddhist where with the Buddhist; there is detachment from the world. "Where Underhill struck new ground was in her insistence that this state of union produced a glorious and fruitful creativeness, so that the mystic who attains this final perfectness is the most active doer - not the reclusive dreaming lover of God." (http://en.wikipedia.org/wiki/Evelyn_Underhill)

Our reading for this day from the book of Wisdom includes the following. "Though she is but one, she can do all things, and while remaining in herself, she renews all things; in every generation she passes into holy souls and makes them friends of God, and prophets" (7:27).

Evelyn Underhill is one of those souls. She is an infusion of mysticism and with it, genuine feminism into His church. True feminism is meek and wise. True feminism asks for the water of life from the bridegroom Jesus Christ.

"If you then, being evil, know how to give good gifts to your children, how much more will *your* heavenly Father give the Holy Spirit to those who ask Him?" (Luke 11:13, NASB).

FLORENCE LAKE JOHN MUIR WILDERNESS

STEWARDS OF THE MYSTERIES OF GOD

"Let a man regard us in this manner, as servants of Christ and stewards of the mysteries of God." (1ST Corinthians 4:1, NASB)

Although St. Paul spoke as an apostle, I believe it is the charge to all those in Holy Orders. The verse essentially outlines the "General Orders" for the clergy of the Church of Jesus Christ. I used the term General Orders because in the military all recruits must memorize and obey the rules of a sentry. A sentry is someone expected to stand guard at a post and be responsible for that area.

As stewards of the mysteries of God, we are charged to care for and to pass on these mysteries to the next generation. What are these mysteries? The mysteries are the truths once delivered to the Saints. "Beloved, while I was making every effort to write you about our common salvation, I felt the necessity to write to you appealing that you contend earnestly for the faith which was once for all handed down to the saints. For certain persons have crept in unnoticed, those who were long beforehand marked out for this condemnation, ungodly persons who turn the grace of our God into licentiousness and deny our only Master and Lord, Jesus Christ." (Jude 3-4, NASB).

The central truths of the faith <u>are</u> the mysteries of God. If you examine the Nicene Creed carefully, it is not just doctrine or even dogma. At its foundation, it is truth as mystery received by faith. We believe that God created everything that exists, even the things we cannot see. We believe that Jesus Christ is both God and a perfect man born conceived by God and born of a Virgin. We believe that He was crucified and died as a sacrifice on our behalf. We believe that Jesus Christ came back to life as predicted and ascended bodily into Heaven and will return to establish an eternal Kingdom that will include us. We believe in one God Who Is also the Holy Spirit Who is the Giver of life. There is one Church and one baptism.

The Christian Church is a Church of Mystery. It is miraculous and mystical. It also is the Spiritual, meeting the material, in the Sacraments and in the incarnation of Jesus Christ. The

Church began at Pentecost and is awaiting the return of Her Bridegroom Jesus Christ.

What we cannot fully explain, we may not adjust to suit our understanding. These mysteries are perceived by faith, affirmed by the faithful throughout generations and authenticated by God the Holy Spirit. These truths are the breath of the Holy Spirit and blood of Jesus Christ flowing through His Body the Church. "God is spirit, and those who worship Him must worship in spirit and truth." (John 4:24, NASB).

THE DIDACHE: THE FIRST CATECHISM

The Didache (Training), written in the early first century, may have existed earlier as oral tradition and the author is unknown. The Didache was well known to the early fathers and accepted by some as Apocrypha but not as part of the New Testament canon. It is older than the canonical Gospels and developed independently from them.

"This Didache reveals more about how Christians saw themselves and how they lived their everyday lives than any book in the Christian Scriptures." (A. Milavec, "The Didache", ix, 2003).

The Didache is divided into five sections with almost half in section one (1) which deals with the "way of life". The focus of the Didache was on Christian formation in a pagan world. Thus there is less emphasis on doctrine (which was still developing) and more on reformation of conduct. My intention is to briefly cover some of the main points of sections one (1:1-6:2) and two (6:3-11-2). This is approximately the first two thirds of the total content.

1:1 "There are two ways: one of life and one of death!" Thus begins the Didache which sounds a lot like the following from Deuteronomy, "I call heaven and earth to witness against you today, that I have set before you life and death, the blessing and the curse. So choose life in order that you may live, you and your descendants." (30:19).

The way of life is defined as loving God and loving neighbor and the golden rule stated in the negative. This is also followed by a brief narrative possibly taken from portions of the Sermon on the Mount. The second rule deals with the commandments and adds six more. This is probably because many of the new converts were pagans not Jews.

1. You will not practice magic.
2. You will not be involved in potions (drugs).
3. You will not murder offspring by means of abortion.
4. You will not kill infants.
5. You will not corrupt boys.
6. You will not have illicit sex.

In addition there were rules for changing speech, attitude and cautions for vigilance that specific minor sins could lead to greater sins. All of this was guided by a spiritual mentor. The final admonition was a "warning against Innovators" (Ibid. p.61). There was also an opportunity for Reconciliation and this may have been a prototype of the Sacrament of Penance.

Section two deals with The Lord's Prayer which should be prayed three times a day and was possibly used as template much like we have for our prayers of the people. Fasting was encouraged and a preference for "flowing water" baptism in the name of the Father, Son and Holy Spirit. Those who were not baptized were not allowed to participate in the Eucharist.

The Eucharist was celebrated with the bread and wine being consecrated by the celebrant and following the prayers of the celebrant, the itinerant "Prophets" would offer prayers as led by the Spirit for as long as the Spirit gave them utterance. Some of the comments about prophets indicate that they were not always trustworThy. It is possible that this eventually became the Preaching.

Much of Catechesis today focuses on the doctrines of the Church which continued to develop toward and find agreement in the ecumenical Church Councils that also determined the canon of Scripture. As the West becomes increasingly pagan and less Christian, we may find that the conduct trained into converts in the Didache, may need to be combined with the Orthodox doctrine of the church in Catechesis. The commandments of the Didache are a stunning reminder of the extent to which the pagan world has found its way into the contemporary church. Amen

WHAT MUST I DO TO BE SAVED?

"Sirs, what must I do to be saved?" They said, "Believe in the Lord Jesus, and you will be saved."(Acts, 30b-31a, NASB)

There are two obvious questions that flow from this passage. What is the jailer asking to be saved from and who is going to do it? Although theologians may quibble with me about this, salvation, conversion and being born again is essentially the same. Because of original sin, humans are born estranged from and enemies of God. It does not matter what the jailer meant with his question because the answer of Paul and Silas understood it to mean saved from eternal separation from God. *Salvation is obtained by turning over our will and life to Jesus Christ.* Salvation is both a specific event and it is ongoing. ("… work out your salvation with fear and trembling." (Phil. 2:12b, NASB). The specific event is often referred to as a "Decision for Christ". We usually think of Christ the Son as the one and only way to God the Father which is correct but Peter's Confession, "You are the Christ, the Son of the living God" is followed by this statement from Jesus. "Jesus said to him, 'Blessed are you, Simon Barjona, because flesh and blood did not reveal this to you, but My Father who is in heaven.'" (Matt. 16:17, NASB). It is God the Father, God the Son and God the Holy Spirit who all witness to us about each other and themselves.

I believe human hearts are prepared by God through Holy Scripture, events (good and bad), the lives and witness of Christians and the beckoning of the Holy Spirit to call upon Christ for salvation. God creates a hunger for Him in our hearts that only He can fill. A good example of this preparation of the heart is when Phillip is prompted by the Holy Spirit to approach an Ethiopian official who happened to be reading a prophesy from the Old Testament about Christ at the same moment (Acts 8:26-40).

When Paul states in Romans, "All who call upon the name of the Lord will be saved." (Romans 10:13), it is not intended as a formula for salvation but a believing response to the Gospel message. The Gospel message offers us an opportunity to believe that *Jesus Christ is who He says that He is and His redemptive sacrifice of Himself on the cross applies to all humans in general and you and me in particular. Finally, it is a turning over your life to His authority*. In this we are reconciled to God and restored to relationship with Him. All Christians are prodigals who have been reconciled to God the Father through the person and work of Christ and the Witness of the Holy Spirit.

I think the key decision for most folks does not begin with a "yes" to the existence of a God. At some level most believe that there is a God. Many folks begin with unbelief in the person and work of Christ but a desire to believe. Here the desire (will) to believe demonstrates that God has already begun a work in the heart of the individual. Others may call out to Christ, like the father of the demoniac, "Lord I do believe, help my unbelief." (Mark 9:24b, NASB) Christ asks all of us the following question. "Who do you say that I am?" Thomas the doubter finally stated, "My Lord and my God" (John 20:28) to the resurrected

Christ. Is this your answer also? I pray that God would give you the faith to receive the truth of this message. Amen.

"There is salvation in no one else; for there is no other name under heaven that has been given among men by which we must be saved." (Acts 4:12, NASB).

ONLY IN REMEMBRANCE OF ME?

"For I have received of the Lord that which also I delivered unto you, that the Lord Jesus the same night in which He was betrayed took bread: And when He had given thanks, He brake it, and said, Take, eat: this is My body, which is broken for you: this do in remembrance of Me. After the same manner also He took the cup, when He had supped, saying, this cup is the new testament in My blood: this do ye, as oft as ye drink it, in remembrance of Me." (1st Corinthians 11:23-25, KJV).

As a Baptist, I remember the table at the front of the church with the words "In remembrance of me". I always understood as they passed out the little cup of grape juice and the plate of bread crumbs, and we ate them, we would remember Jesus. There was no reference to the table as an altar (although they had altar calls every Sunday).

There is a sensibleness and certainty to reformed theology which also extends to the empty cross. We didn't sacrifice Christ on the Altar (Nor do the Liturgical Churches) and we didn't have to put Him back on the cross. Jesus was not in the communion elements and a crucifix was so off putting. That's what those Catholics believed…and those Lutherans….and those Anglicans…..and those Orthodox.

"This is the bread which cometh down from heaven, that a man may eat thereof, and not die. I am the living bread which came down from heaven: if any man eat of this bread, he shall live for ever: and the bread that I will give is My flesh, which I will give for the life of the world. The Jews therefore strove among themselves, saying, How can this man give us his flesh to eat? Then Jesus said unto them, Verily, verily, I say unto you, Except ye eat the flesh of the Son of man, and drink His blood, ye have no life in you. Whoso eateth my flesh, and drinketh my blood, hath eternal life; and I will raise him up at the last day. For my flesh is meat indeed, and my blood is drink indeed. He that eateth my flesh, and drinketh my blood, dwelleth in me, and I in him. As the living Father hath sent me, and I live by the Father: so he that eateth me, even he shall live by me. This is that bread which came down from heaven: not as your fathers did eat manna, and are dead: he that eateth of this bread shall live forever. (John 6:50-58)

Eucharistic Prayer A (Holy Eucharist Rite II BCP)

The people remain standing. The Celebrant, whether bishop or priest, faces them and sings or says

The Lord be with you.

People And also with you.
Celebrant Lift up your hearts.
People We lift them to the Lord.
Celebrant Let us give thanks to the Lord our God.
People It is right to give him thanks and praise.

Then, facing the Holy Table, the Celebrant proceeds

It is right, and a good and joyful thing, always and everywhere to give thanks to you, Father Almighty, Creator of heaven and earth. Therefore we praise you, joining our voices with Angels and Archangels and with all the company of heaven, who for ever sing this hymn to proclaim the glory of your Name:

Celebrant and People

Holy, Holy, Holy Lord, God of power and might, heaven and earth are full of your glory.
Hosanna in the highest.
Blessed is he who comes in the name of the Lord.
Hosanna in the highest.

The people stand or kneel.

Then the Celebrant continues

Holy and gracious Father: In your infinite love you made us for yourself, and, when we had fallen into sin and become subject to evil and death, you, in your mercy, sent Jesus Christ, your only and eternal Son, to share our human nature, to live and die as one of us, to reconcile us to you, the God and Father of all.

He stretched out his arms upon the cross, and offered himself, in obedience to your will, a perfect sacrifice for the whole world.

At the following words concerning the bread, the Celebrant is to hold it, or lay a hand upon it; and at the words concerning the cup, to hold or place a hand upon the cup and any other vessel containing wine to be consecrated.

On the night he was handed over to suffering and death, our Lord Jesus Christ took bread; and when he had given thanks to you, he broke it, and gave it to his disciples, and said, "Take, eat: This is my Body, which is given for you. Do this for the remembrance of me."

After supper he took the cup of wine; and when he had given thanks, he gave it to them, and said, "Drink this, all of you: This is my Blood of the new Covenant, which is shed for you and for many for the forgiveness of sins. Whenever you drink it, do this for the remembrance of me."

Therefore we proclaim the mystery of faith:

Celebrant and People

Christ has died.
Christ is risen.
Christ will come again.

The Celebrant continues

We celebrate the memorial of our redemption, O Father, in this sacrifice of praise and thanksgiving. Recalling his death, resurrection, and ascension, we offer you these gifts.

Sanctify them by your Holy Spirit to be for your people the Body and Blood of your Son, the holy food and drink of new and unending life in him. Sanctify us also that we may faithfully receive this holy Sacrament, and serve you in unity, constancy, and peace; and at the last day bring us with all your saints into the joy of your eternal kingdom.

All this we ask through your Son Jesus Christ: By him, and with him, and in him, in the unity of the Holy Spirit all honor and glory is yours, Almighty Father, now and forever. *AMEN*.

No matter what is preached from the pulpit on any given Sunday, the Great Thanksgiving in the Liturgy always contains the Gospel. Amen

UT OMNES UNUM SINT (THAT THEY ALL MAY BE ONE)

"Hear O Israel, the Lord is our God, the Lord is One" (Deuteronomy 6:4, NASB).

"That they may all be one; even as You, Father, *are* in Me and I in You, that they also may be in Us, so that the world may believe that You sent Me." (John 17:21, NASB).

"And when the day of Pentecost was fully come, they were all with one accord in one place." Acts 2:1, NASB).

So the Father is God, the Son is God, and the Holy Ghost is God. And yet they are not three Gods but one God. (The Creed of Athanasius)

"We believe in one holy catholic and apostolic Church." (from the Nicene Creed).

"By Him and with Him, and in Him, in the unity of the Holy Spirit all honor and glory is Yours, Almighty Father, now and forever. AMEN. (Eucharistic Doxology).

"*There is* one body and one Spirit, just as also you were called in one hope of your calling; one Lord, one faith, one baptism." (Eph. 4:4-5, NASB).

"A new commandment I give to you, that you love one another, even as I have loved you, that you also love one another. By this all men will know that you are My disciples, if you have love for one another." (John 13:34-35, NASB)

"We can do nothing well till we act 'with one accord'; we can have no accord in action till we agree together in heart; we cannot agree without a supernatural influence; we cannot have a supernatural presence unless we pray for it; we cannot pray acceptably without repentance and confession. Our Church's strength would be irresistible, humanly speaking, were it but at unity with itself." (from Tract number 90 by John Henry Newman 1841).

"O God the Father of our Lord Jesus Christ, our only Savior, the Prince of Peace: Give us grace seriously to lay to heart the great dangers we are in by our unhappy divisions; take away all hatred and prejudice, and whatever else may hinder us from godly union and concord; that, as there is but one Body and one Spirit, one hope of our calling, one Lord, one Faith, one Baptism, one God and Father of us all, so we may be all of one heart and of one soul, united in one holy bond of truth and peace, of faith and charity, and may with one mind and one mouth glorify *thee*; through Jesus Christ our Lord. *Amen*." (BCP, 'For the Unity of the Church' p.818).

NEAR VOGELSANG HIGH SIERRA CAMP, YOSEMITE

MOUNTAINS

"Great is the LORD, and highly to be praised,

And His greatness is unsearchable.

One generation shall praise Your works to another,

And shall declare Your mighty acts.

On the glorious splendor of Your majesty

And on Your wonderful works, I will meditate.

Men shall speak of the power of Your awesome acts,

And I will tell of Your greatness.

They shall eagerly utter the memory of Your abundant goodness

And will shout joyfully of Your righteousness." (Psalm 145: 3-7)

Mountains are frequently associated with God in the Holy Scriptures. Often it is a pivotal time in the history of God's people. Noah's Ark came to rest on *Mount Ararat*. Abraham took his son Isaac to *Mount Moriah* intending to sacrifice him. *Mt Moriah* is also the site of Solomon's Temple. *Mt Sinai* (Horeb) was where God revealed Himself to Moses and where the Ten Commandments were given. It was *Mount Nebo* where Moses struck the rock to provide water. It was *Mount Zion* where David built his palace and it was the *Mount of Olives* where Jesus delivered His sermon and where He was arrested. *Mount Tabor* is traditionally understood to be the place of His transfiguration. Even one of God's names, El Shaddai can be translated "God of the Mountain". (NJB)

I was born and raised in Michigan where my family also visited the Porcupine Mountains near Lake Superior in the Upper Peninsula. As a child they seemed imposing at about 1,600' of elevation. In the mid 1960's a friend of mine Dan McCosh and I drove to California from Michigan in June and I saw mountains, real mountains, for the first time. As we approached Loveland, Colorado, the Rockies emerged immediately and abruptly from the plains. My heart nearly stopped as we anticipated driving over Loveland Pass at nearly 12,000'. My hands immediately began to sweat. There was still considerable snow along the sides of the road as we crossed the Continental Divide. This view of the Rocky Mountains approaching Loveland made such an indelible impression on me that I knew someday I would live in an area where I could view and travel in God's glorious mountains.

Now, in my twentieth year in Fresno CA, when the air is clear I can see much of the central Sierra Nevada Mountains. The mountains offer year round recreation and I am there once a week. There is no way to describe how my spirit is elevated each time I drive east into the mountains to begin a new adventure with friends or in the company of my Airedales Susie and Duke who change from pets to companions who especially enjoy the winter snow. I also spent four of the best days of my life with my sons as we backpacked a portion of the John Muir Trail together. Hearing them talking together as men around a campfire as I fell asleep in my tent was as beautiful a sound as any waterfall or river.

These mountain places are where I fellowship with God too for it was He who made these things and us also. It can at times be as intimate an occasion for me as when I proclaim the words of the Great Thanksgiving during the Holy Eucharist.

Climb the mountains and get their good tidings. Nature's peace will flow into you as sunshine flows into trees. The winds will blow their own freshness into you, and the storms their energy, while cares will drop off like autumn leaves. ~John Muir

MARATHONS

"Therefore, since we have so great a cloud of witnesses surrounding us, let us also lay aside every encumbrance and the sin which so easily entangles us, and let us run with endurance the race that is set before us" (Hebrews 12:1, NASB)

I quit smoking in 1983 and gained twenty pounds within the next couple of months. Exercise can be an effective behavioral substitute for smoking and I began walking. My first mile took eighteen and a half minutes and I thought I was going to have a heart attack at the end. I began walking daily and decided on the goal of running for a mile. After this, it was a 5K then a 10K run. Making progress in one area of life can keep one optimistic even when other areas are less than satisfactory. As a side effect, my weight diminished. Eventually I ran (and walked) my first marathon in six hours twenty minutes at age 48. I finished last behind a lady who had to give up her moniker "Last Place Grace". I used a marathon training plan by Jeff Galloway.

Since that time I have run over one hundred marathons and ultra-marathons (for me, everything worth doing is worth overdoing). Because of occasional overuse injuries, I later learned to mix running with swimming and biking and have remained relatively injury free since adopting this method of training. I must also say that I am physically unremarkable and did not participate in school sports. <u>I personally believe that</u>

<u>completing a marathon as a runner or a "double century" as a cyclist is a breakthrough experience that can forever positively impact a person's life.</u>

Let me now discuss what can happen along the way. Either of these or similar goals requires dedication and discipline from the individual. These are goals arrived at only incrementally and over time, often in the company of individuals with which you will forge lifelong friendships. These are goals which require patience, persistence and focus. These are goals that require priority setting and boundary setting. Perhaps the most important thing these goals require is self-discipline or self-regulation. Along the way one gains a sense of self efficacy and respect for one's own body. Food is seen as fuel not something to appease a mood. Sweat comes from places a shower never reaches and physical fatigue helps one sleep better.

If you find that your schedule is overwhelming and that you can't seem to get closure on things, maybe it is a self-regulation issue and not the demands of your work. Goal setting and attainment require the skills one must acquire to complete a marathon. Time management and task accountability are problems I continue to see with professionals who even have masters and doctoral level preparation. If you are a Christian and your life is still a chaotic mess, then maybe a marathon is in order. Run two and call me in the morning.

"Therefore I run in such a way, as not without aim; I box in such a way, as not beating the air." (1st Corinthians 9:26, NASB).

THE FISHERMAN

"And He said to them, 'Cast the net on the right-hand side of the boat and you will find *a catch*.' So they cast, and then they were not able to haul it in because of the great number of fish." (John 21:6, NASB)

Some of my earliest memories of my father are the kind shared by my brother Don, a fellow conscript. They are war stories nearly of the magnitude of "Two Years Before The Mast" with my father in the role of Captain Thompson. I can still see his unshaven face, his nearly bald head, topped by his requisite fishing cap (he had a special cap for each occasion) and his white fake Meerschaum Kaywoodie pipe projecting from the corner of his mouth. You could hear a periodic crackle of hot spit as he puffed away on the Bond Street Tobacco.

My galley slave name on these expeditions was "Right Oar". My Brother was eight years older with the compliment of my name, "Left Oar". My dad called out for two right oar strokes for every one left oar stroke to keep from going in circles. This was called "trolling". I would eventually tire and say to my dad, "Can't we 'still' fish?" He would reply, "We're still fishing". When we eventually did still fish, it seemed like the 14 foot aluminum boat became a solar cooker with us in it. "Dad the fish aren't biting, can't we move on?" He would always retort, "That means the "Big Ones" are moving in, we're going to land a lunker Bass any minute. Of course my dad would get "Buck Fever" (I know this is usually reserved for deer hunting but he always used the phrase when anyone got nervous) when a lunker got on and usually found a way of losing the six pound fish by breaking twelve pound test line.

For lunch, we had sandwiches made by my father with a handful of "padada chips" and a semi cold "Pop" (that's what we called soft drinks in Michigan). Eventually we would convince my dad to allow us to row to shore and he would finish the day by himself. Everyone else had at least a 3 HP Evinrude outboard motor but dad said you couldn't sneak up on the lunkers with an outboard motor. Lots of bass in Tipsico Lake knew enough to take cover when they heard the loud unlubricated oar locks squeaking with each oar stroke or the banging of his Kawoodie pipe on the side of the boat to knock out old tobacco. I still have the pen knife he used to scrape the inside of his pipe.

He would return after dark with his lantern flashing to warn other boats and then clean his "mess" of fish under the same lantern light, brushing away mosquitoes from his face. The "victory" garden was the repository for the waste. He once gave my mother a fly rod for her birthday which was unnecessary since she didn't fish and refused to be shanghaied with my brother and me. We had a plaque on the wall with a skeleton holding a fishing pole over the side of a boat with the caption, "stubborn cuss". That was my dad.

And where did we go on vacation? Well, of course we went fishing at a cabin. I can hear my mother now, "Milton this is not a vacation for me, just a more primitive place to cook and clean." To this day because of my father, I have more stories than you can shake a stick at. Life was much simpler and funnier back then. I wish I could tell him how God has blessed me the past few years. It would be so much better if he were here. I miss him so. Amen

And He said to them, "Follow Me, and I will make you fishers of men." (Matt. 4:19, NASB).

THE CHURCH AND THE HOMELESS: QUESTIONS FOR OUR TIME

"And Jesus said to him, 'The foxes have holes and the birds of the air *have* nests, but the Son of Man has nowhere to lay His head.'" (Luke 9:58)

I was once impressed by a local church that had a sign reading, "The mission field begins at the edge of our property." The reality for our church is that the mission field begins on our church campus. Part of our church outreach is to the homeless in our community. We offer dinners twice weekly, operate a thrift shop, limited financial assistance and minister to the homeless. Our deacons direct this ministry on campus and there is additional involvement by our parishioners in the Poverello House, a privately funded ecumenical facility in another part of Fresno. http://www.poverellohouse.org/social.html.

Perhaps the thing that rends my heart the most is the erosion of human dignity and personal freedom that results from a life lived on the streets. They are more likely to be the victims of crimes, less likely to receive adequate medical services and like fast food wrappers thrown from a car window; they too are blown into the gutters.

Most research on the homeless includes *lack of affordable housing* as a major contributing factor. The problem with this phrase is that it can be misleading. For most homeless individuals who generally have no employment, they would at a minimum need rent subsidies and at a maximum need free housing.

Even though they are a part of our church, they generally self-select for the "outer court". They are a family unto themselves with only a few participating in our main services. During Morning Prayer I can look out the window and see individuals sleeping in our shrubbery. During Evening Prayer, I have seen men gather outside the chapel on a circular bench and pass a bottle around but they do not attend the service. They are not passing through our campus. It has become their home. Some receive mail there and make calls from our receptionist's phone. Do we add a Portable Potty and hire a security guard for overnight? What is the range and scope of our assistance?

I believe they feel secure on our campus but as their numbers increase the staff and volunteers feel less secure. How do we incorporate them into the life of the church? How we help them is as important as the fact that we offer help. How do we say like Jesus, "Get up and walk"? How do we teach them to fish not just hand them fish? How do we reach them spiritually so that they may be transformed by the love of Christ?

Like the Good Samaritan, how can we dress their wounds, accompany them to a destination, pay for their lodging and care but leave them at some point? Like a good parent, how do we help them to become independent and capable of self-governance and self-support? How do we equip them as any other of the Saints? I believe it has become an ever expanding issue for us. Is this an issue for your church also?

How we respond is a measure of our understanding of the grace given us. Amen

www.ingramcontent.com/pod-product-compliance
Lightning Source LLC
LaVergne TN
LVHW051118080426
835510LV00018B/2100

Blood Money
The Method and Madness of Assassins

by RJ Parker

Blood Money: The Method and Madness of Assassins